McGraw-Hill Mathematics

Transition Handbook

Bridge the Gaps!

What Do I Need to Know?

Skill Builder

Challenge

Teacher Guide

2

McGraw-Hill School Division

New York   Farmington

McGraw-Hill School Division 🪐

A Division of The **McGraw·Hill** *Companies*

Copyright © McGraw-Hill School Division,
a Division of the Educational and Professional Publishing Group of The McGraw-Hill Companies, Inc.
All rights reserved. Permission granted to reproduce for use with McGraw-Hill MATHEMATICS.

McGraw-Hill School Division
Two Penn Plaza
New York, New York 10121-2298

Printed in the United States of America

ISBN 0-02-100204-5 / 2

3 4 5 6 7 8 9 066 05 04 03 02

GRADE 2 Contents

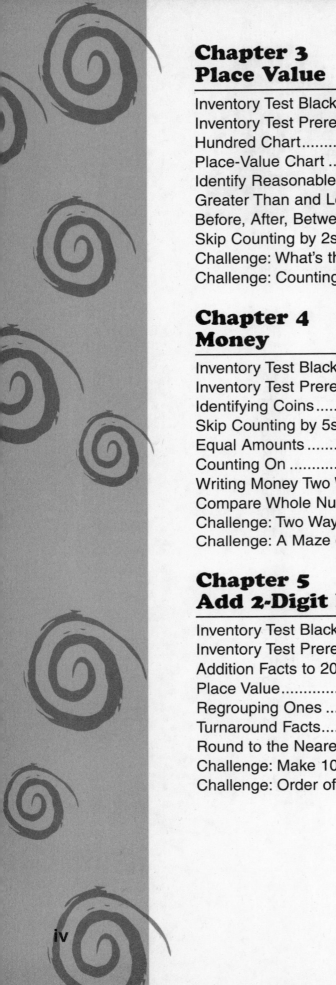

Chapter 3
Place Value

Chapter 4
Money

Chapter 5
Add 2-Digit Numbers

Chapter 6
Subtract 2-Digit Numbers

Chapter 7
Time

Chapter 8
Data and Graphs

Chapter 9
Measurement

Chapter 10
Geometry

Chapter 11
Fractions and Probability

Chapter 12
Place Value to 1,000

Chapter 13
Add and Subtract 3-Digit Numbers

Chapter 14
Multiplication and Division

To the Teacher

Welcome to *McGraw-Hill Mathematics Transition Handbook: Bridge the Gaps!* The goal of these materials is to provide assessment and instruction in the prerequisite skills that some of your students need to be successful in math at this grade level.

For each chapter of the *McGraw-Hill Mathematics* student text, there is a 2-page inventory test called *What Do I Need To Know?* You will find these inventory tests as blackline masters on the A and B pages in this Teacher Guide. The results of the tests will help you diagnose any gaps in student knowledge. You can then provide students with materials needed to reteach or challenge them as appropriate.

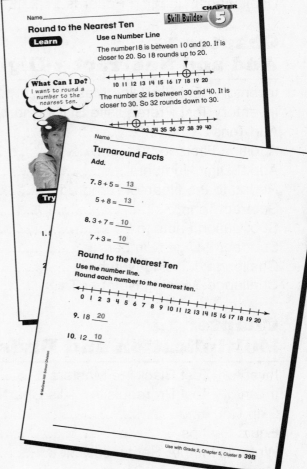

The charts found on the C and D pages following the blackline masters will prescribe a special *Skill Builder* lesson in the handbook for each test item that a student answers incorrectly.

The *Skill Builder* lessons are presented in language that is simple and direct. The lessons are highly visual and have been designed to keep reading to a minimum.

The Learn section begins with a student asking *What Can I Do?* This section provides stepped-out models and one or more strategies to help bridge any gaps in the student's knowledge. Following this is *Try It*, a section of guided practice, and *Power Practice*, a section containing exercises to ensure that your students acquire the math power they need to be successful in each chapter of their mathematics textbook.

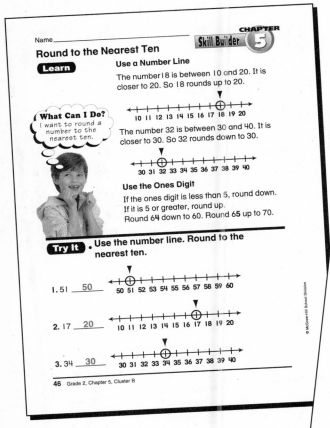

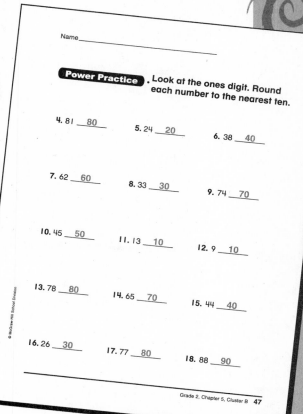

Two *Challenge* activities appear at the end of each chapter in the handbook. These provide a variety of math experiences for students who had no difficulty with the inventory test. Students will enjoy working on the puzzles, riddles, codes, and other more challenging formats. The *Challenge* activities will provide an opportunity for your more advanced students to work independently, allowing you to focus attention on those who need additional instruction before they work on the lessons in their math text.

Name_____

Make 100

Find two numbers that add up to 100.
Color them red.

Find two more.
Color them blue.

Continue until you have colored 10 pairs of numbers.
Share your number sentences with the class.

1	2	3	4	5	6	7	8	9	10
11	12	13	14	15	16	17	18	19	20
21	22	23	24	25	26	27	28	29	30
31	32	33	34	35	36	37	38	39	40
41	42	43	44	45	46	47	48	49	50
51	52	53	54	55	56	57	58	59	60
61	62	63	64	65	66	67	68	69	70
71	72	73	74	75	76	77	78	79	80
81	82	83	84	85	86	87	88	89	90
91	92	93	94	95	96	97	98	99	100

Possible answers include 1 + 99, 2 + 98, 3 + 97, . . ., 41 + 49.

1. ____ + ____ = 100
2. ____ + ____ = 100
3. ____ + ____ = 100
4. ____ + ____ = 100
5. ____ + ____ = 100
6. ____ + ____ = 100
7. ____ + ____ = 100
8. ____ + ____ = 100
9. ____ + ____ = 100
10. ____ + ____ = 100

Name_____

Order of Addition
Draw pictures.
Then add.

8 + 9 = __17__

9 + 8 = __17__

5 + 7 = __12__

7 + 5 = __12__

**Use what you learned.
Add.**

15 + 12 = 27

24 + 42 = 66

38 + 19 = 57

384 + 6 = 390

444 + 138 = 582

12 + 15 = __27__

42 + 24 = __66__

19 + 38 = __57__

6 + 384 = __390__

138 + 444 = __582__

The Teacher Guide provides a complete lesson plan for each *Skill Builder* and *Challenge*. Each *Skill Builder* lesson plan includes a lesson objective, *Getting Started* activities, teaching suggestions, and questions to check the student's understanding. There is also a section called *What If the Student Can't*, which offers additional activities in case a student needs more support in mastering an essential prerequisite skill or lacks the understanding needed to complete the *Skill Builder* exercises successfully.

At least one *Skill Builder* lesson plan in each chapter has a feature called *Learn with Partners & Parents*. This activity is intended for students to use at home with parents or siblings or at school with a classmate-partner to practice a math skill in a game-like setting.

The lesson plan for each *Challenge* includes a lesson objective along with suggestions for introducing and using the *Challenge*.

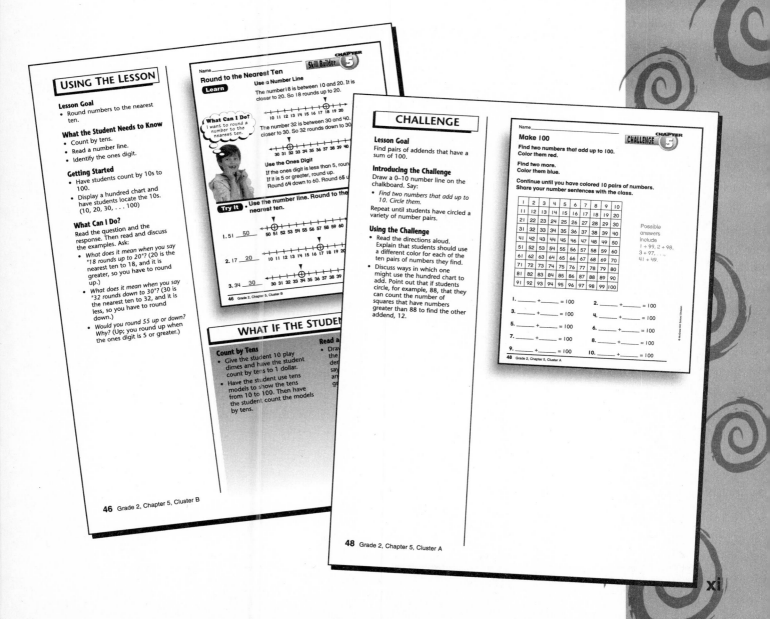

Number Line

Write each missing number.

1.
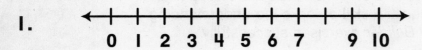
0 1 2 3 4 5 6 7   9 10

_____

2.
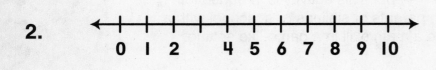
0 1 2   4 5 6 7 8 9 10

_____

Compare Numbers

Use the number line. Circle the greater number.

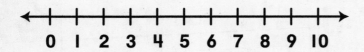
0 1 2 3 4 5 6 7 8 9 10

3. 6   7

4. 9   4

Addition

Add.

5. $4 + 3 =$ _____

6. $\begin{array}{r} 3 \\ + 4 \\ \hline \end{array}$

Addition Facts to 8

Add.

7. 2 + 5 = _____

8.　　4
　　　+ 4
　　　‾‾‾‾

Subtraction Facts to 8

Subtract.

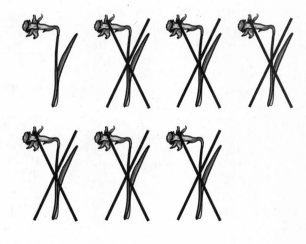

9. 8 − 1 = _____

10.　7
　　　− 6
　　　‾‾‾‾

CHAPTER 1 PRE-CHAPTER ASSESSMENT

Assessment Goal
This two-page assessment covers skills identified as necessary for success in Chapter 1 Addition and Subtraction Strategies and Facts to 12. The first page assesses the major prerequisite skills for Cluster A. The second page assesses the major prerequisite skills for Cluster B. When the Cluster A and Cluster B prerequisite skills overlap, the skill(s) will be covered in only one section.

Getting Started
- Allow students time to look over the two pages of the assessment. Point out the labels that identify the skills covered.
- Have students find math vocabulary terms used in the assessment. List vocabulary terms on the board as students identify them. If necessary, review the meanings of all essential math vocabulary.

Introducing the Assessment
- Explain to students that these pages will help you know if they are ready to start a new chapter in their math textbooks.
- Students who have transferred from another school may not have been introduced to some of these skills. Encourage students to do their best and assure them you will help them learn any needed skills.

Cluster A Challenge
Those students who demonstrate mastery of the skills on this page will not need to use the reteaching worksheets. Instead, these students can do the Cluster A Challenge found on page 10.

Name _____

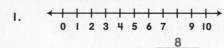

Number Line
Write each missing number.

1.

0 1 2 3 4 5 6 7 __ 9 10
         8

2.
0 1 2 __ 4 5 6 7 8 9 10
    3

Compare Numbers
Use the number line. Circle the greater number.

0 1 2 3 4 5 6 7 8 9 10

3. 6 (7)   4. (9) 4

Addition
Add.

5. $4 + 3 = $ ___7___   6. $\begin{array}{r} 3 \\ + 4 \\ \hline 7 \end{array}$

© McGraw-Hill School Division

1A Use with Grade 2, Chapter 1, Cluster A

CLUSTER A PREREQUISITE SKILLS

The skills listed in this chart are those identified as major prerequisite skills for students' success in the lessons in Cluster A of the chapter. Each skill is covered by one or more assessment items as shown in the middle column. The right column provides the page numbers for the lessons in this book that reteach the Cluster A prerequisite skills.

Skill Name	Assessment Items	Lesson Pages
Number Line	1-2	2
Compare Numbers	3-4	3
Addition	5-6	4-5

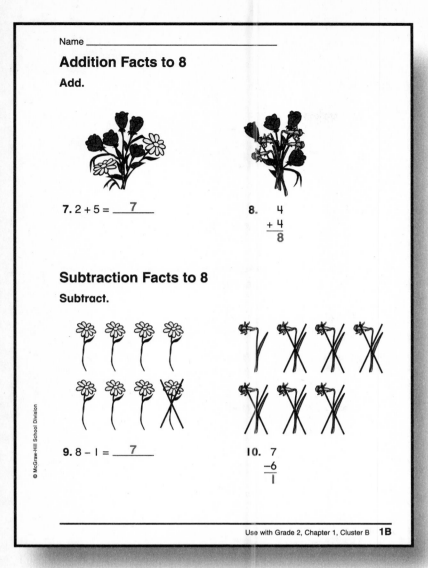

Name _____

Addition Facts to 8

Add.

7. 2 + 5 = ___7___

8.   4
        + 4
        ———
          8

Subtraction Facts to 8

Subtract.

9. 8 − 1 = ___7___

10.   7
         − 6
         ———
           1

CLUSTER B PREREQUISITE SKILLS

The skills listed in this chart are those identified as major prerequisite skills for students' success in the lessons in Cluster B of the chapter. Each skill is covered by one or more assessment items as shown in the middle column. The right column provides the page numbers for the lessons in this book that reteach the Cluster B prerequisite skills

Skill Name	Assessment Items	Lesson Pages
Addition Facts to 8	7-8	6-7
Subtraction Facts to 8	9-10	8-9

CHAPTER 1 PRE-CHAPTER ASSESSMENT

Alternative Assessment Strategies

- Oral administration of the assessment is appropriate for younger students or those whose native language is not English. Read the skills title and directions one section at a time. Check students' understanding by asking them to tell you how they will do the first exercise in the group.

- For some skill types you may wish to use group administration. In this technique, a small group or pair of students complete the assessment together. Through their discussion, you will be able to decide if supplementary reteaching materials are needed.

Intervention Materials

If students are not successful with the prerequisite skills assessed on these pages, reteaching lessons have been created to help them make the transition into the chapter.

Item correlation charts showing the skills lessons suitable for reteaching the prerequisite skills are found beneath the reproductions of each page of the assessment.

Cluster B Challenge

Those students who demonstrate mastery of the skills on this page will not need to use the reteaching worksheets. Instead, these students can do the Cluster B Challenge found on page 11.

Lesson Goal

- Count on and back on a number line.

What the Student Needs to Know

- Count by 1s.
- Recognize the meanings of "greater" and "less."

Getting Started

Draw a 0–10 number line on the chalkboard. Cover up the number 3. Say:

- *Read the numbers. Which number is missing?* (3)

Repeat, covering a different number.

What Can I Do?

Read the question and the response. Then read and discuss the examples. Ask:

- *When you count on, are the numbers greater or less?* (greater) *In which direction do you move on the number line?* (right)
- *When you count back, are the numbers greater or less?* (less) *In which direction do you move on the number line?* (left)

Try It

- Suggest that students look to the left and right of the number that is missing. To find the number, they could count on from the number to the left or count back from the number to the right.
- Have students check their work by counting from 0 to 10.

Power Practice

- Review the columns of the chart before students begin, and make sure they know where to write the numbers that are 1 less and 1 more.
- Have students complete the practice items. Discuss their answers.

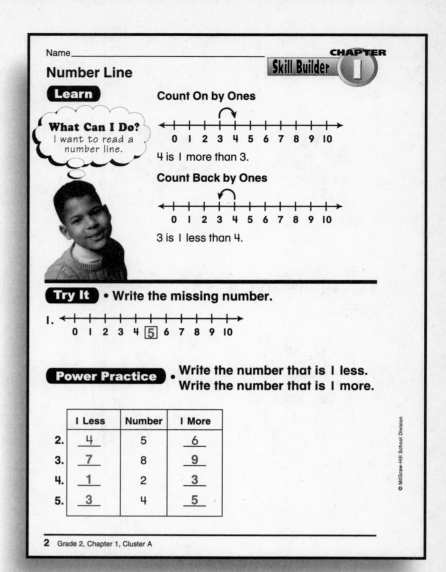

Name_____

Number Line

Learn

What Can I Do? I want to read a number line.

Count On by Ones

0 1 2 3 4 5 6 7 8 9 10

4 is 1 more than 3.

Count Back by Ones

0 1 2 3 4 5 6 7 8 9 10

3 is 1 less than 4.

Try It • Write the missing number.

1. 0 1 2 3 4 [5] 6 7 8 9 10

Power Practice • Write the number that is 1 less.
Write the number that is 1 more.

	I Less	Number	I More
2.	4	5	6
3.	7	8	9
4.	1	2	3
5.	3	4	5

© McGraw-Hill School Division

2 Grade 2, Chapter 1, Cluster A

WHAT IF THE STUDENT CAN'T

Count by 1s

- Line up groups of ten students.
- Have students "count off" by 1s.
- Ask students to realign themselves and count off again. Repeat.

Recognize the Meanings of "Greater" and "Less"

- Give the student ten counters and number cards 0–10.
- Have the student pick two cards, model the numbers with counters, and identify which number is greater and which is less.

Complete the Power Practice

- Discuss each incorrect answer. Point out that the numbers in column 1 are supposed to be 1 less, and the numbers in column 3 are supposed to be 1 more. Have the student use a number line to determine the correct answers.
- Have the student read the corrected answers using this wording: "4 is 1 less than 5. 6 is 1 more than 5."

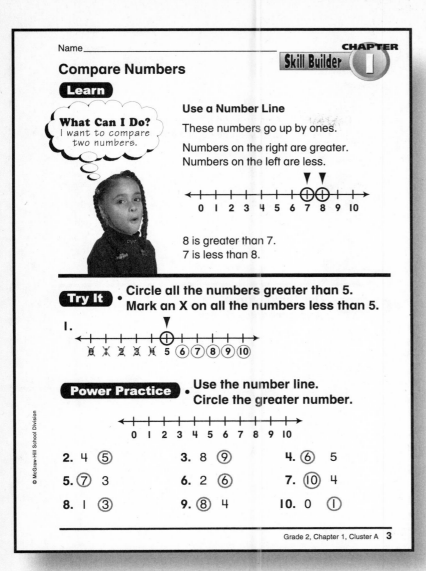

Compare Numbers

Learn

What Can I Do?
I want to compare two numbers.

Use a Number Line

These numbers go up by ones.

Numbers on the right are greater.
Numbers on the left are less.

▼ ▼
+—+—+—+—+—+—+—⊕—⊕—+—+
0 1 2 3 4 5 6 7 8 9 10

8 is greater than 7.
7 is less than 8.

Try It • **Circle all the numbers greater than 5.**
• **Mark an X on all the numbers less than 5.**

1.
▼
+—+—+—+—+—+—⊕—+—+—+—+
0̷ 1̷ 2̷ 3̷ 4̷ 5 ⑥ ⑦ ⑧ ⑨ ⑩

Power Practice • **Use the number line.**
• **Circle the greater number.**

+—+—+—+—+—+—+—+—+—+—+
0 1 2 3 4 5 6 7 8 9 10

2. 4 ⑤   3. 8 ⑨   4. ⑥ 5

5. ⑦ 3   6. 2 ⑥   7. ⑩ 4

8. 1 ③   9. ⑧ 4   10. 0 ①

Grade 2, Chapter 1, Cluster A **3**

WHAT IF THE STUDENT CAN'T

Recognize the Meanings of "Greater" and "Less"

• Divide a pile of counters unevenly between two students.

• Have the pair guess which one has the greater number and which one has the lesser number.

• Have students count to confirm their guesses. Repeat.

Read a Number Line

• Mark off a 0–10 number line using masking tape on the floor.

• Have students locate the numbers you say aloud by standing on them.

• Have students move left or right to find numbers that are greater or less than the one you assigned them.

Complete the Power Practice

• Discuss each incorrect answer. Have student pairs work together to locate each number on the number line and determine which number comes before (further left) and after (further right). Remind them that numbers on the right are greater.

Lesson Goal

• Compare numbers 0–10.

What the Student Needs to Know

• Recognize the meanings of "greater" and "less."

• Read a number line.

Getting Started

Have students count aloud from 0 to 10. Ask:

• *Which number is the greatest?* (10)

What Can I Do?

Read the question and the response. Then read and discuss the example. Ask:

• *If 8 is to the right of 7, which number is greater?* (8)

• *If 6 is to the left of 7, which number is less?* (6)

Try It

After the directions are read aloud, students may follow these steps:

• Find 5. Look to the right. Those numbers are greater than 5. Circle them.

• Find 5. Look to the left. Those numbers are less than 5. Mark an X on them.

Power Practice

• Have students complete the practice items. Then review each answer, having volunteers use this wording: "5 is greater than 4."

Lesson Goal
- Add facts to 8 horizontally or vertically.

What the Student Needs to Know
- Recognize plus and equal signs.
- Draw a picture to match a number sentence.

Getting Started
On the chalkboard, draw a row of 3 Xs next to a row of 4 Xs. Say:

- *How many Xs are in the first group? (3) How many are in the second group? (4) How many Xs are there in all? (7)*

Erase the row of Xs and redraw them as a row of 3 Xs above a row of 4 Xs. Ask:

- *How many Xs are in the first group? (3) How many are in the second group? (4) How many Xs are there in all? (7) Does it matter if the groups are across or down? (no)*

What Can I Do?
Read the question and the response. Then read and discuss the example. Ask:

- *What is the difference between the first 2 + 3 example and the second 2 + 3 example? (One is written across, and the other is written down.)*

- *What is the difference in the answers? (There is no difference; the answers are the same.)*

Have volunteers come to the chalkboard and draw their own across and down pictures for the example 2 + 3.

Try It
Read the directions aloud. Make sure students understand that adding across or down yields the same answer.

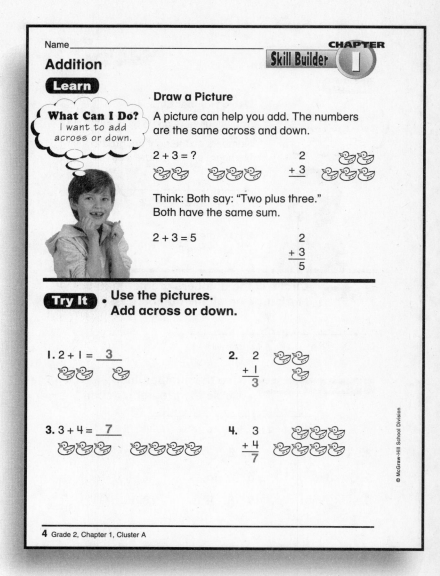

Name_____

CHAPTER 1

Skill Builder

Addition

Learn

What Can I Do? I want to add across or down.

Draw a Picture
A picture can help you add. The numbers are the same across and down.

$2 + 3 = ?$

$\begin{array}{r} 2 \\ + 3 \end{array}$

Think: Both say: "Two plus three." Both have the same sum.

$2 + 3 = 5$

$\begin{array}{r} 2 \\ + 3 \\ \hline 5 \end{array}$

Try It • Use the pictures. Add across or down.

1. $2 + 1 = \underline{\ 3\ }$

2. $\begin{array}{r} 2 \\ + 1 \\ \hline 3 \end{array}$

3. $3 + 4 = \underline{\ 7\ }$

4. $\begin{array}{r} 3 \\ + 4 \\ \hline 7 \end{array}$

4 Grade 2, Chapter 1, Cluster A

WHAT IF THE STUDENT CAN'T

Recognize Plus and Equal Signs
- Write a variety of addition number sentences on the chalkboard and have the student read them aloud.
- Write number sentences with circles in place of the plus and equal signs. For example:

  2 ☐ 4 ☐ 6

Have the student supply the signs and read the sentences aloud.

Draw a Picture to Match a Number Sentence
- Supply counters and have the student model a given number sentence using counters first. Then have the student draw or trace the counters.

Power Practice • Add. If you need to, draw a picture.

5. $2 + 6 =$ __8__

6.
$$\begin{array}{r} 2 \\ + 6 \\ \hline 8 \end{array}$$

7. $1 + 4 =$ __5__

8.
$$\begin{array}{r} 1 \\ + 4 \\ \hline 5 \end{array}$$

9. $3 + 0 =$ __3__

10.
$$\begin{array}{r} 3 \\ + 0 \\ \hline 3 \end{array}$$

11. $5 + 3 =$ __8__

12.
$$\begin{array}{r} 5 \\ + 3 \\ \hline 8 \end{array}$$

© McGraw-Hill School Division

USING THE LESSON

Power Practice
- After students have completed the problems, volunteers may share the drawings they used to solve them.
- Ask students to tell whether they find it easier to add across or down. Remind them that the answer is the same either way. If they have trouble adding across, they can always rewrite the number sentence as a vertical exercise.

Learn with Partners and Parents
Students can use plastic spoons and forks to set up horizontal and vertical addition problems. Have them follow these steps.
- Choose two numbers to add, from 0–4.
- Model the numbers with forks and spoons. Place the models across or down.
- Write an addition sentence or a vertical problem to match the fork-and-spoon model. Find the sum.

WHAT IF THE STUDENT CAN'T

Complete the Power Practice
- Have the students identify the exercises that should have the same answers. (5 and 6; 7 and 8; 9 and 10; 11 and 12)

- Discuss each incorrect answer. Have the student use counters to model any fact he or she missed.

Lesson Goal
- Add facts to 8.

What the Student Needs to Know
- Find one more.
- Draw a picture to match a number sentence.

Getting Started
Line up three students on one side of the room and three on the other side. Ask:

- *How many students are in the first group? (3) How many students are in the second group? (3)*

Move one student from group 2 to group 1. Say:

- *3 and 1 more is 4.*

Continue moving one student at a time. Then ask:

- *How many students are there in all? (6) So 3 + 3 = 6.*

What Can I Do?
Read the question and the response. Then read and discuss the examples. Ask:

- *What are the numbers being added in the first example? (4 and 2)*
- *What are the numbers being added in the second example? (2 and 5)*
- *How can drawing a picture help you add? (You can count the items in the picture to find the sum.)*
- *If you had to solve the number sentence 3 + 4, what would you draw to help you find the sum? (You would draw a group of 3 items and a group of 4 items.)*

Try It
Point out that students may use the pictures to help them add. Alternatively, they may count on to find the sums.

WHAT IF THE STUDENT CAN'T

Find One More
- Supply counters and number cards 0–9. Have the student pick a card, model the number with counters, and then find one more using a counter. Once the student is comfortable modeling one more, have the student try finding one more without the counters.

Draw a Picture to Match a Number Sentence
- Write a variety of addition facts on the board, and have the student tell how many objects he or she would draw. For example, given the number sentence 3 + 2 = ?, the student should respond that he or she would draw a group of 3 items and a group of 2 items.

Name_____

Power Practice • Add. Count on or draw a picture.

5. 3 + 3 = __6__   **6.** 1 + 5 = __6__

7. 2 + 3 = __5__   **8.** 3 + 4 = __7__

9.   5   **10.**   3
     + 2   + 5
     ———   ———
       7   8

11.   2   **12.**   6
      + 6   + 1
      ———   ———
        8   7

USING THE LESSON

Power Practice

- Tell students that it is up to them to decide whether it is easier for them to draw a picture or count on to add. If they do not need to use either strategy, they may add on their own.
- Volunteers may share any drawings they used to solve the problems.

WHAT IF THE STUDENT CAN'T

Complete the Power Practice
- Have the student discuss the strategy he or she used to find each sum.

- Discuss each incorrect answer. Have the student model with counters any fact he or she missed.

Lesson Goal
• Subtract facts to 8.

What the Student Needs to Know
• Find one less.
• Draw a picture to match a subtraction sentence.

Getting Started
Line up five students in the front of the classroom. Ask:
• *How many students are in the group?* (5)

Have one student sit down. Say:
• *5 and 1 less is 4.*

Have another student sit down. Then ask:
• *How many students sat down?* (2) *How many students are left?* (3) *So 5 – 2 = 3.*

What Can I Do?
Read the question and the response. Then read and discuss the examples. Ask:
• *Why do you start subtracting with the greater number?* (You can't subtract a greater number from a lesser number; you are subtracting a lesser number from a greater number.)
• *Why is 7 – 1 – 1 the same as 7 – 2?* (Subtracting 2 is the same as subtracting 1 twice.)
• *If you had to solve the number sentence 4 – 3, what would you draw? What would you cross out?* (You would draw a group of 4 items and cross out 3 of them.)

Name_____

CHAPTER **Skill Builder** **1**

Subtraction Facts to 8

Learn

What Can I Do? I want to subtract from numbers up to eight.

Count Back
Start with the greater number.
Count back to find the difference.

7 – 2 = ?

Think: 7 and 1 less is 6, and 1 less is 5.

Draw a Picture
Use a picture to help you subtract.

4 – 1 = ?

Draw 4 circles. Cross out 1 circle.

○ ○ ○ ⊗

Count the circles that are left to find the difference.

Try It • Subtract.

1. 2 – 1 = __1__

   ▢ ⊠

2. 6
   – 3
   ——
   3

3. 7 – 3 = __4__

   △ △ △ △ ⊠ ⊠ ⊠

4. 3
   – 0
   ——
   3

   ○ ○ ○

WHAT IF THE STUDENT CAN'T

Find One Less
• On the board, draw a 0–10 number line. Supply number cards 1–10. Have students pick a number, point to the number on the number line, and move their fingers back one to find one less. Once students are competent at this skill, have them use the number cards without the number line.

Draw a Picture to Match a Subtraction Sentence
• Give students several subtraction sentences, such as the following:

  7 – 5 = 2
  6 – 2 = 4
  8 – 3 = 5

Have the student use connecting cubes or counters to model each sentence. Then ask him or her to draw a picture to represent each sentence. You may want students to work in pairs, taking turns modeling with counters and drawing pictures.

Name_____

Power Practice • Subtract. Count back or use a picture.

5. 8 – 2 = __6__

6. 5 – 3 = __2__

△ △ △ △ △

7. 2 – 2 = __0__

○ ○

8. 7 – 4 = __3__

☆ ☆ ☆ ☆ ☆
☆ ☆

9.
  6   △ △ △
– 2   △ △ △
―――
  4

10.
  3   □ □ □
– 2
―――
  1

11.
  8   ☆ ☆ ☆ ☆
– 5   ☆ ☆ ☆ ☆
―――
  3

12.
  4   ○ ○ ○ ○
– 3
―――
  1

Try It

Explain that the pictures show the subtraction problems. The number of things in all is the number of things shown in the picture. The number of things subtracted is the number of things crossed out in the pictures. Students may use the picture or the count back strategy to find each answer.

Power Practice

• Tell students that if they do not need to use either strategy, they may subtract on their own.

• Suggest that students check their work by adding. Give them this example: 8 – 2 = 6; 6 + 2 = 8.

WHAT IF THE STUDENT CAN'T

Complete the Power Practice

• Have the student discuss the strategy he or she used to find each answer.

• Discuss each incorrect answer. Have the student use counters to model any fact he or she missed.

CHALLENGE

Introducing the Challenge

- On the chalkboard, write this addition sentence:

  4 + 1 + 0 + 2 = ?

- Discuss with students how they might go about finding the sum. Some students might add 1 to 4, 0 to that sum, and 2 to that sum. Others might add numbers in pairs, 4 + 1 and 0 + 2, and then add that sum. Explain that numbers in an addition problem may be added in any order.

Using the Challenge

- Read the directions aloud. Explain that students are to estimate and guess the greatest sum before doing the addition.

- Have students add to check their guesses. If necessary, students may use counters to check their work.

- Interested students might enjoy working together to prepare a similar worksheet for their classmates.

Addition Paths

Can you guess which path has the greatest sum? Circle it. Then add each path to check your guess.

10 Grade 2, Chapter 1, Cluster A

Name_____

Make 5

How many ways can you make 5?
Write each missing number and sign.

$0 + 5 = 5$ $5 - 0 = 5$

$1 \boxed{+} \boxed{4} = 5$ $6 - 1 = 5$

$2 \boxed{+} \boxed{3} = 5$ $7 \boxed{-} \boxed{2} = 5$

$3 \boxed{+} \boxed{2} = 5$ $8 \boxed{-} \boxed{3} = 5$

$4 \boxed{+} \boxed{1} = 5$

$5 \boxed{+} \boxed{0} = 5$

© McGraw-Hill School Division

CHALLENGE

Introducing the Challenge

- On the chalkboard, write these number sentences:

  $2 + 1 = 3$ $5 - 2 = 3$

- Explain that both sentences you wrote are ways of making 3. Ask:
- *Can you think of another addition sentence that makes 3? Can you think of another subtraction sentence that makes 3?* (Possible answers include 0 + 3, 1 + 2, 3 + 0; 3 – 0, 4 – 1, 6 – 3, and so on.)

Using the Challenge

- Read the directions aloud. Remind students that they can use both plus and minus signs.
- Some students may benefit from using counters to complete the worksheet.
- Challenge students who enjoyed this activity to list ten number sentences that make 4.

Add and Subtract One

Add or subtract.

1. 8 + 1 = _____

2. 8 − 1 = _____

3.   4
    − 1
    ‾‾‾

4.   4
    + 1
    ‾‾‾

Tens and Ones

Write each number.

5.

_____

6.

_____

Name_____

Addition and Subtraction Facts to 12

Add or subtract.

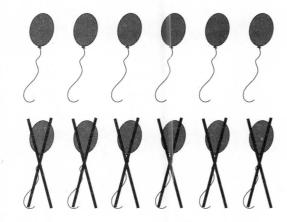

7. $12 - 6 =$ _____

8. $\begin{array}{r} 6 \\ + 6 \\ \hline \end{array}$

Write a Number Sentence

Write a number sentence to match each picture.

9. _____ + _____ = _____

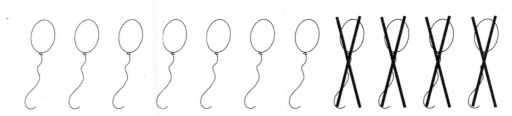

10. _____ ◯ _____ ◯ _____

Assessment Goal

This two-page assessment covers skills identified as necessary for success in Chapter 2 Addition and Subtraction Strategies and Facts to 20. The first page assesses the major prerequisite skills for Cluster A. The second page assesses the major prerequisite skills for Cluster B. When the Cluster A and Cluster B prerequisite skills overlap, the skill(s) will be covered in only one section.

Getting Started

- Allow students time to look over the two pages of the assessment. Point out the labels that identify the skills covered.
- Have students find math vocabulary terms used in the assessment. List vocabulary terms on the board as students identify them. If necessary, review the meanings of all essential math vocabulary.

Introducing the Assessment

- Explain to students that these pages will help you know if they are ready to start a new chapter in their math textbooks.
- Students who have transferred from another school may not have been introduced to some of these skills. Encourage students to do their best and assure them you will help them learn any needed skills.

Cluster A Challenge

Those students who demonstrate mastery of the skills on this page will not need to use the reteaching worksheets. Instead, these students can do the Cluster A Challenge found on page 18.

Name_____

CHAPTER 2 What Do I Need To Know?

Add and Subtract One

Add or subtract.

1. $8 + 1 =$ ___9___

2. $8 - 1 =$ ___7___

3.
$$\begin{array}{r} 4 \\ -\ 1 \\ \hline 3 \end{array}$$

4.
$$\begin{array}{r} 4 \\ +\ 1 \\ \hline 5 \end{array}$$

Tens and Ones

Write each number.

5. _____13_____

6. _____12_____

11A Use with Grade 2, Chapter 2, Cluster A

CLUSTER A PREREQUISITE SKILLS

The skills listed in this chart are those identified as major prerequisite skills for students' success in the lessons in Cluster A of the chapter. Each skill is covered by one or more assessment items as shown in the middle column. The right column provides the page numbers for the lessons in this book that reteach the Cluster A prerequisite skills.

Skill Name	Assessment Items	Lesson Pages
Add and Subtract One	1-4	12
Tens and Ones	5-6	13

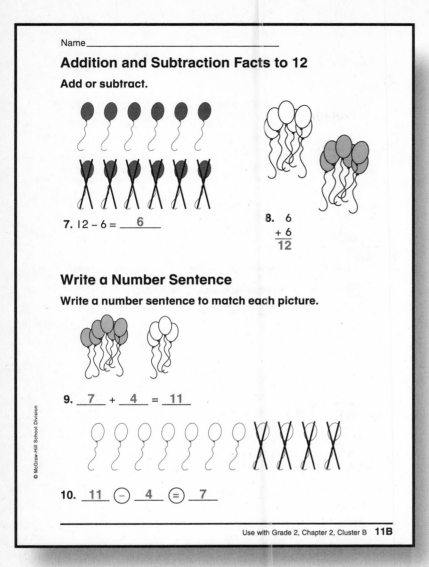

Name_____

Addition and Subtraction Facts to 12

Add or subtract.

7. $12 - 6 =$ ___6___

8.
$$\begin{array}{r} 6 \\ + 6 \\ \hline 12 \end{array}$$

Write a Number Sentence

Write a number sentence to match each picture.

9. ___7___ + ___4___ = ___11___

10. ___11___ (−) ___4___ (=) ___7___

© McGraw-Hill School Division

CLUSTER B PREREQUISITE SKILLS

The skills listed in this chart are those identified as major prerequisite skills for students' success in the lessons in Cluster B of the chapter. Each skill is covered by one or more assessment items as shown in the middle column. The right column provides the page numbers for the lessons in this book that reteach the Cluster B prerequisite skills

Skill Name	Assessment Items	Lesson Pages
Addition and Subtraction Facts to 12	7-8	14-15
Write a Number Sentence	9-10	16-17

CHAPTER 2 PRE-CHAPTER ASSESSMENT

Alternative Assessment Strategies

- Oral administration of the assessment is appropriate for younger students or those whose native language is not English. Read the skills title and directions one section at a time. Check students' understanding by asking them to tell you how they will do the first exercise in the group.

- For some skill types you may wish to use group administration. In this technique, a small group or pair of students complete the assessment together. Through their discussion, you will be able to decide if supplementary reteaching materials are needed.

Intervention Materials

If students are not successful with the prerequisite skills assessed on these pages, reteaching lessons have been created to help them make the transition into the chapter.

Item correlation charts showing the skills lessons suitable for reteaching the prerequisite skills are found beneath the reproductions of each page of the assessment.

Cluster B Challenge

Those students who demonstrate mastery of the skills on this page will not need to use the reteaching worksheets. Instead, these students can do the Cluster B Challenge found on page 19.

Lesson Goal
• Add and subtract one.

What the Student Needs to Know
• Count to ten.
• Read a number line.

Getting Started
Have students count aloud from 0 to 10. Then have them count backward from 10 to 0.

What Can I Do?
Read the question and the response. Then read and discuss the examples. Ask:
• *How could you write "7 and 1 more" as a number sentence?*
  $(7 + 1 = 8)$
• *How could you write "7 and 1 less" as a number sentence?*
  $(7 - 1 = 6)$

Try It
Students might follow these steps:
• Find the first number on the number line. Put your finger there.
• To add 1, move your finger to the right one space. To subtract 1, move your finger to the left one space.

Power Practice
• Have students complete the practice items. Then review each answer.

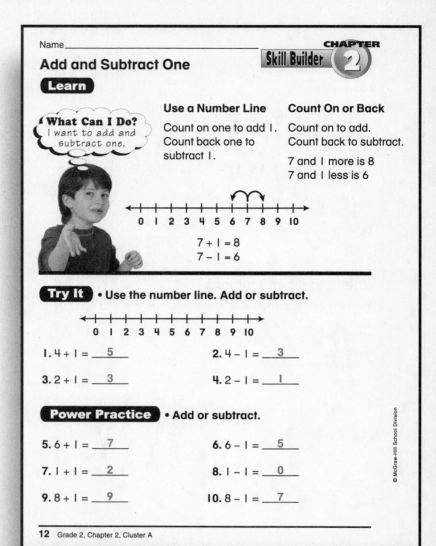

Name_____

Add and Subtract One

Learn

What Can I Do? I want to add and subtract one.

Use a Number Line
Count on one to add 1.
Count back one to subtract 1.

Count On or Back
Count on to add.
Count back to subtract.

7 and 1 more is 8
7 and 1 less is 6

0 1 2 3 4 5 6 7 8 9 10

$7 + 1 = 8$
$7 - 1 = 6$

Try It • Use the number line. Add or subtract.

0 1 2 3 4 5 6 7 8 9 10

1. $4 + 1 =$ __5__   2. $4 - 1 =$ __3__

3. $2 + 1 =$ __3__   4. $2 - 1 =$ __1__

Power Practice • Add or subtract.

5. $6 + 1 =$ __7__   6. $6 - 1 =$ __5__

7. $1 + 1 =$ __2__   8. $1 - 1 =$ __0__

9. $8 + 1 =$ __9__   10. $8 - 1 =$ __7__

© McGraw-Hill School Division

12 Grade 2, Chapter 2, Cluster A

WHAT IF THE STUDENT CAN'T

Count to Ten
• Mix number cards 0–10 and have the student line them up in order.
• Place a number of counters between 1 and 10 on the student's desk. Ask the student to count them.

Read a Number Line
• Draw a 0–10 number line on the chalkboard. Omit some of the numbers and have the student write them.

• Draw a 0–10 number line on the chalkboard. Say one of the numbers and have the student name the number that comes just before and just after that number.

Complete the Power Practice
• Discuss each incorrect answer. Use counting on and counting back on a number line to help students see their errors: *6 + 1 is the same as 6 and 1 more = 7. 6 – 1 is the same as 6 and 1 less = 5.*

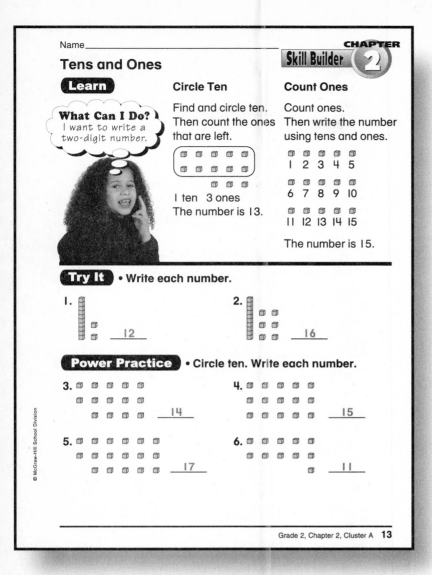

Name_____

Tens and Ones

Learn

What Can I Do?
I want to write a two-digit number.

Circle Ten

Find and circle ten. Then count the ones that are left.

1 ten 3 ones
The number is 13.

Count Ones

Count ones. Then write the number using tens and ones.

1 2 3 4 5
6 7 8 9 10
11 12 13 14 15

The number is 15.

Try It • Write each number.

1. ___12___

2. ___16___

Power Practice • Circle ten. Write each number.

3. ___14___

4. ___15___

5. ___17___

6. ___11___

© McGraw-Hill School Division

Grade 2, Chapter 2, Cluster A **13**

WHAT IF THE STUDENT CAN'T

Count Ten Items
- Place ten counters in a line. Have the student count them. Mix the counters and place them out in random order. Have the student count them again.
- Find opportunities to have the student count a variety of classroom objects to 10. For example, you may ask the student to count pencils, crayons, books, sheets of paper, and so on.

Identify Tens and Ones
- Write these numbers in a place-value chart: 12, 15, 18. Have the student identify the number of tens and ones in each number.

- Play Place-Value Bingo with students. Instead of calling out a number such as "12," call out "1 ten, 2 ones" and have students mark the appropriate number. Be sure the numbers on the prepared Bingo cards fall within the range of 0–19. Continue with calls such as "2 ones," "1 ten," "6 ones," and so on.

Complete the Power Practice
- Discuss each incorrect answer. Look for common errors such as reversed place value or incorrect counting.
- Have students show each number with tens and ones models.

USING THE LESSON

Lesson Goal
- Write two-digit numbers.

What the Student Needs to Know
- Count ten items.
- Identify tens and ones.

Getting Started
Display a tens model and a ones model. Ask:
- *Which model stands for 1 one? Which model stands for 1 ten? What number do the models stand for when I put them together?* (11)

What Can I Do?
Read the question and the response. Then read and discuss the examples. Ask:
- *What number has 1 ten and 2 ones?* (12) *1 ten and 3 ones?* (13) *1 ten and 4 ones?* (14)
- *What is the least number you can make that has a tens digit and a ones digit?* (10)

Try It
Students who are having trouble might try counting on from 10 before they write the number.

Power Practice
- Point out that students may circle any 10 ones to make 1 ten.
- Have students complete the practice items and share their answers.

Lesson Goal
- Add and subtract facts to 12.

What the Student Needs to Know
- Draw a picture to match a number sentence.
- Recognize plus and minus signs.
- Add doubles.

Getting Started
Choose 10 students to come to the front of the room. Ask:
- *How many ways can you arrange yourselves to make 2 groups?*

Have volunteers count the students to find the number in each group and write the resulting addition sentence.

What Can I Do?
Read the question and the response. Then read and discuss the examples. Ask:
- *When you put two groups together, are you adding or subtracting?* (adding)
- *When you take some items away from a group, are you adding or subtracting?* (subtracting)
- *You want to solve the problem 12 – 5. Why would it help to find the answer to 10 – 5 first?* (If you know the answer to 10 – 5 = 5, then adding 2 to the answer would solve the problem 12 – 5.)

Try It
You may wish to have students circle the signs before they begin their computations.

Power Practice
- Tell students that it is up to them to decide whether it is easier for them to draw a picture or use facts they already know. If they do not need to use either strategy, they may add and subtract on their own.
- Volunteers may share any drawings they used to solve the problems.

Name_____

Addition and Subtraction Facts to 12

Learn

Draw a Picture
A picture can help you add or subtract.

4 + 6 = ?

What Can I Do?
I forgot an addition or subtraction fact!

The plus sign means add. 4 + 6 = 10

$$\begin{array}{r} 11 \\ -\ 3 \\ \hline 8 \end{array}$$

The minus sign means subtract. 11 – 3 = 8

Use Facts You Know
You forgot 12 – 5. You know 10 – 5 = 5.
Think: 12 is 2 more than 10.
12 – 5 must be 2 more than 10 – 5.
So, 12 – 5 = 7.

Try It • Watch the signs. Add or subtract.

1. 2 + 9 = __11__

2. $$\begin{array}{r} 12 \\ -\ 8 \\ \hline 4 \end{array}$$

3. 9 – 7 = __2__

4. $$\begin{array}{r} 3 \\ +\ 7 \\ \hline 10 \end{array}$$

WHAT IF THE STUDENT CAN'T

Draw a Picture to Match a Number Sentence
- Write related addition and subtraction facts on the board and have students first model each one with counters and then draw a picture for each. For example, you might write 5 + 6 = ? and 11 – 6 = ?

Recognize Plus and Minus Signs
- Write a variety of addition and subtraction number sentences on the chalkboard and have students read them aloud. Then have students add or subtract to solve the problem.
- Write addition and subtraction number sentences on the board. Ask students to circle the sign in each addition sentence. Repeat the activity asking the students to circle the sign in each subtraction sentence. Then have students add or subtract to solve the problem.

Name_____

5. 2 + 7 = __9__

6.
$$\begin{array}{r} 5 \\ + 6 \\ \hline 11 \end{array}$$

7. 11 − 4 = __7__

8.
$$\begin{array}{r} 8 \\ + 4 \\ \hline 12 \end{array}$$

9. 10 − 9 = __1__

10.
$$\begin{array}{r} 9 \\ - 4 \\ \hline 5 \end{array}$$

11. 5 + 7 = __12__

12.
$$\begin{array}{r} 11 \\ - 6 \\ \hline 5 \end{array}$$

© McGraw-Hill School Division

Learn with Partners & Parents

Play a game of Concentration to review and reinforce addition and subtraction facts to 12.

- Write each of these facts on a card: 1 + 2, 3 − 0, 2 + 2, 9 − 5, 0 + 5, 12 − 7, 2 + 4, 11 − 5, 6 + 1, 10 − 3, 3 + 5, 12 − 4, 6 + 3, 11 − 2.

- Players mix the cards and lay them face down. The first player turns up two cards. If their answers are the same, the player keeps the cards and goes again. If not, the player replaces the cards, and the next player has a turn.

- When all cards have been picked, the player with the most pairs wins.

WHAT IF THE STUDENT CAN'T

Add Doubles

- Make flash cards with doubles from 1 + 1 to 6 + 6. Have students work in pairs to practice adding doubles.

Complete the Power Practice

- Have students discuss the strategy they used to find each sum or difference.

- Discuss each incorrect answer. Have the student model any fact he or she missed using counters.

Lesson Goal

• Write an addition or subtraction number sentence to match a picture.

What the Student Needs to Know

• Recognize plus and minus signs.
• Count objects in an array.

Getting Started

On the board, draw a group of 3 circles and a group of 5 circles. Ask:

• *Would I add or subtract to find how many in all?* (add)

Write: $3 + 5 = 8$

Cross out 3 circles. Ask:

• *Would I add or subtract to find how many are left?* (subtract)

Write: $8 - 3 = 5$

What Can I Do?

Read the question and the response. Then read and discuss the examples. Ask:

• *What sign do you use to find how many in all?* (plus sign)
• *What sign do you use to find how many are left?* (a minus sign)
• *When you subtract 6 from 10, what number do you write first?* (10) *Why?* (The greater number comes first in a subtraction sentence.)

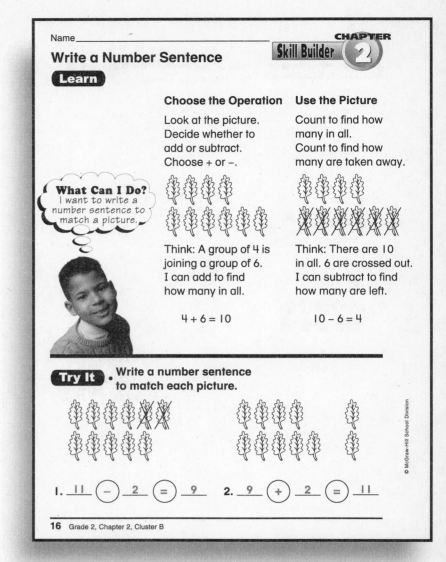

WHAT IF THE STUDENT CAN'T

Recognize Plus and Minus Signs

• Write several addition and subtraction sentences on the board. Ask students to circle the sign in each addition sentence and read the sentence aloud. Repeat the activity, asking students to circle the subtraction signs and read each subtraction sentence. Then have student solve each problem.

Count Objects in an Array

• Place counters in a line. Have the student count them. Mix the counters and place them in an array. Have the student count them again. Repeat with a different number of counters.

Name_____

Power Practice • Write a number sentence to match each picture.

3. __10__ (−) __4__ (=) __6__

4. __6__ (+) __6__ (=) __12__

5. __4__ (+) __7__ (=) __11__

6. __12__ (−) __9__ (=) __3__

Try It

Suggest that students keep the following in mind:

- When there are two groups of items, you should add the groups.
  When there is one group of items and several items are crossed out, you should subtract the items that are crossed out from the total number of items.
- Count the group or groups. Write the numbers on the lines.
- Write = in the second circle.
- Check your number sentence against the picture. Does it make sense?

Power Practice

- Remind students to choose the operation first and to use numbers that correspond to the items in the pictures.
- Have students share their work by reading their addition and subtraction sentences aloud.

WHAT IF THE STUDENT CAN'T

Complete the Power Practice

- Have the student explain how he or she might decide whether to add or subtract.
- Discuss each incorrect answer. Be sure the student understands that when writing subtraction sentences, he or she should count the total number of items and subtract the crossed-out items from that number. Have the student count the objects in each picture to check his or her work.

CHALLENGE

Introducing the Challenge

- On the chalkboard, write these addition sentences:

  $4 + 1 + ? = 8$

  $1 + ? + 5 = 8$

  $3 + 3 + ? = 8$

- Discuss with students how they might go about finding the missing numbers. Possible methods include (1) adding the two given addends and subtracting the sum from the given sum or (2) guessing and checking.

  (Answers are 3, 2, and 2.)

Using the Challenge

- Read the directions aloud.

- Point out that the three numbers alongside each arrow add up to the number in the middle of the puzzle.

- Have the students look at the first puzzle. Ask them to follow along the top arrow. Ask: *What two numbers are given?* (2 and 6) *What addition sentence can they make with these numbers?* ($2 + 6 = 8$) *What number can they subtract from 12 to find the missing number in the top right corner?* (8) *What number sentence shows the subtraction?* ($12 - 8 = 4$) *What number goes in the top right box?* (4)

- Point out that the squares are self-checking. If one answer is correct, it will be correct in both directions, across and down.

CHALLENGE CHAPTER 2

Sum Puzzles

In each puzzle, follow the arrows. The sum of the numbers across or down is the number in the center.

2	6	4
5	12	4
5	3	4

8	1	5
6	14	2
0	7	7

9	0	7
2	16	1
5	3	8

18 Grade 2, Chapter 2, Cluster A

Name_____

Make Up Number Sentences

Look at the picture.

What can you add?
What can you subtract?

Write four number sentences.
Ask a friend to solve them.

1. __11__ (−) __2__ (=) __9__

2. __2__ (−) __1__ (=) __1__

3. __3__ (+) __2__ (=) __5__

4. __1__ (+) __8__ (=) __9__

Answers will vary.
Possible answers are given.

CHALLENGE

Introducing the Challenge

- Give each student up to 12 counters. Say:
- *Count your counters. Write a subtraction sentence that uses the number of counters you have. Then write an addition sentence whose sum is the number of counters you have.*
- Have students share their answers with the class.

Using the Challenge

- Read the directions aloud. Point out that there may be more than four correct answers.
- Tell students to try to write subtraction sentences as well as addition sentences.
- Have students share and explain the sentences they wrote.

Hundred Chart

Fill in the missing numbers.

1.

1	2	3	4	5	6	7	8	9	10
11	12	13	14	15	16	17	18	19	20
21	22	23	24	25	26	27	28	29	
31	32	33	34	35	36	37	38	39	
41	42	43	44	45	46	47	48	49	
51	52	53	54	55	56	57	58	59	
61	62	63	64	65	66	67	68	69	
71	72	73	74	75	76	77	78	79	80
81	82	83	84	85	86	87	88	89	90
91	92	93	94	95	96	97	98	99	100

Place-Value Chart

Write each number.

2.

tens	ones
4	2

_____

3.

tens	ones
1	8

_____

Identify Reasonable Estimates

Circle the best estimate.

4. 1 10 100

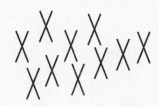

Name_____

Greater Than and Less Than

Circle the number that is greater.

5. 14   16   **6.** 30   3

Before, After, Between

Write the number that comes

7. just after 9. _____

8. between 12 and 14. _____

9. just before 20. _____

Skip Counting by 2s

Fill in the missing numbers.

10.

1	2	3	4	5	6	7	8	9	10
11		13		15		17		19	
21		23		25	26	27	28	29	30
31	32	33	34	35	36	37	38	39	40
41	42	43	44	45	46	47	48	49	50
51	52	53	54	55	56	57	58	59	60
61	62	63	64	65	66	67	68	69	70
71	72	73	74	75	76	77	78	79	80
81	82	83	84	85	86	87	88	89	90
91	92	93	94	95	96	97	98	99	100

Assessment Goal

This two-page assessment covers skills identified as necessary for success in Chapter 3 Place Value. The first page assesses the major prerequisite skills for Cluster A. The second page assesses the major prerequisite skills for Cluster B. When the Cluster A and Cluster B prerequisite skills overlap, the skill(s) will be covered in only one section.

Getting Started

- Allow students time to look over the two pages of the assessment. Point out the labels that identify the skills covered.

- Have students find math vocabulary terms used in the assessment. List vocabulary terms on the board as students identify them. If necessary, review the meanings of all essential math vocabulary.

Introducing the Assessment

- Explain to students that these pages will help you know if they are ready to start a new chapter in their math textbooks.

- Students who have transferred from another school may not have been introduced to some of these skills. Encourage students to do their best and assure them you will help them learn any needed skills.

Cluster A Challenge

Those students who demonstrate mastery of the skills on this page will not need to use the reteaching worksheets. Instead, these students can do the Cluster A Challenge found on page 28.

Name_____

CHAPTER 3 — What Do I Need To Know?

Hundred Chart

Fill in the missing numbers.

1.

1	2	3	4	5	6	7	8	9	10
11	12	13	14	15	16	17	18	19	20
21	22	23	24	25	26	27	28	29	30
31	32	33	34	35	36	37	38	39	40
41	42	43	44	45	46	47	48	49	50
51	52	53	54	55	56	57	58	59	60
61	62	63	64	65	66	67	68	69	70
71	72	73	74	75	76	77	78	79	80
81	82	83	84	85	86	87	88	89	90
91	92	93	94	95	96	97	98	99	100

Place-Value Chart

Write each number.

2.

tens	ones
4	2

42

3.

tens	ones
1	8

18

Identify Reasonable Estimates

Circle the best estimate.

4. 1 (10) 100

X X X
X X X X X
X X X

19A Use with Grade 2, Chapter 3, Cluster A

CLUSTER A PREREQUISITE SKILLS

The skills listed in this chart are those identified as major prerequisite skills for students' success in the lessons in Cluster A of the chapter. Each skill is covered by one or more assessment items as shown in the middle column. The right column provides the page numbers for the lessons in this book that reteach the Cluster A prerequisite skills.

Skill Name	Assessment Items	Lesson Pages
Hundred Chart	1	20-21
Place-Value Chart	2-3	22-23
Identify Reasonable Estimates	4	24

Name_____

Greater Than and Less Than

Circle the number that is greater.

5. 14 (16)

6. (30) 3

Before, After, Between

Write the number that comes

7. just after 9. ___10___

8. between 12 and 14. ___13___

9. just before 20. ___19___

Skip Counting by 2s

Fill in the missing numbers.

10.

1	2	3	4	5	6	7	8	9	10
11	12	13	14	15	16	17	18	19	20
21	22	23	24	25	26	27	28	29	30
31	32	33	34	35	36	37	38	39	40
41	42	43	44	45	46	47	48	49	50
51	52	53	54	55	56	57	58	59	60
61	62	63	64	65	66	67	68	69	70
71	72	73	74	75	76	77	78	79	80
81	82	83	84	85	86	87	88	89	90
91	92	93	94	95	96	97	98	99	100

© McGraw-Hill School Division

Use with Grade 2, Chapter 3, Cluster B **19B**

CLUSTER B PREREQUISITE SKILLS

The skills listed in this chart are those identified as major prerequisite skills for students' success in the lessons in Cluster B of the chapter. Each skill is covered by one or more assessment items as shown in the middle column. The right column provides the page numbers for the lessons in this book that reteach the Cluster B prerequisite skills

Skill Name	Assessment Items	Lesson Pages
Greater Than and Less Than	5-6	25
Before, After, Between	7-9	26
Skip Counting by 2s	10	27

Alternative Assessment Strategies

- Oral administration of the assessment is appropriate for younger students or those whose native language is not English. Read the skills title and directions one section at a time. Check students' understanding by asking them to tell you how they will do the first exercise in the group.

- For some skill types you may wish to use group administration. In this technique, a small group or pair of students complete the assessment together. Through their discussion, you will be able to decide if supplementary reteaching materials are needed.

Intervention Materials

If students are not successful with the prerequisite skills assessed on these pages, reteaching lessons have been created to help them make the transition into the chapter.

Item correlation charts showing the skills lessons suitable for reteaching the prerequisite skills are found beneath the reproductions of each page of the assessment.

Cluster B Challenge

Those students who demonstrate mastery of the skills on this page will not need to use the reteaching worksheets. Instead, these students can do the Cluster B Challenge found on page 29.

USING THE LESSON

Lesson Goal
- Count to 100.

What the Student Needs to Know
- Count to 10.
- Order numbers.
- Compare numbers.

Getting Started
Have students count aloud from 0 to 10. Ask:
- *Which is greater, 8 or 9?* (9) *Which is less, 5 or 6?* (5)
- *Put these numbers in order: 4, 3, 5.* (3, 4, 5) *Put these numbers in order: 8, 10, 9.* (8, 9, 10)

What Can I Do?
Read the question and the response. Then read and discuss the examples. Ask:
- *What is true of all the numbers in the first column of the hundred chart?* (The ones digit is 1.)
- *What is true of all the numbers in the last column of the hundred chart?* (The ones digit is 0.)
- *If you move your finger down any column, how do the numbers change?* (They increase by 10.)

Name_____

 CHAPTER 3

Hundred Chart

Learn

What Can I Do?
I don't remember some numbers to 100.

Find Patterns in a Hundred Chart
Here are the first three rows of a hundred chart.

1	2	3	4	5	6	7	8	9	10
11	12	13	14	15	16	17	18	19	20
21	22	23	24	25	26	27	28	29	30

A hundred chart shows the order of numbers. It shows number patterns, too.
How can the chart help you count by 10s?
How can it help you count by 5s?
How can you tell which numbers are greater?
How can you tell which numbers are less?

Try It • Fill in the missing numbers.

I.

1	2	3	4	5	6	7	8	9	10
11	12	13	14	15	16	17	18	19	**20**
21	22	23	24	25	26	27	28	29	**30**
31	32	33	34	35	36	37	38	39	**40**
41	42	43	44	45	46	47	48	49	**50**
51	52	53	54	55	56	57	58	59	**60**
61	62	63	64	65	66	67	68	69	70
71	72	73	74	75	76	77	78	79	80
81	82	83	84	85	86	87	88	89	90
91	92	93	94	95	96	97	98	99	100

20 Grade 2, Chapter 3, Cluster A

WHAT IF THE STUDENT CAN'T

Count to 10
- Place a number of counters between 1 and 10 on the student's desk. Ask the student to count them.
- Provide opportunities for the students to help distribute classroom materials by counting out items, such as 10 pencils, crayons, scissors, and so on.

Order Numbers
- Distribute number cards 0–10 and have students mix them and line them up in order.

Name_____

Power Practice • Fill in the missing numbers.

2.

1	2	3	4	5	6	7	8	9	10
11	12	13	14	**15**	16	17	18	19	20
21	22	23	24	**25**	26	27	28	29	30
31	32	33	34	**35**	36	37	38	39	40
41	42	43	44	**45**	46	47	48	49	50
51	52	53	54	**55**	56	57	58	59	60
61	62	63	64	**65**	66	67	68	69	70
71	72	73	74	**75**	76	77	78	79	80
81	82	83	84	**85**	86	87	88	89	90
91	92	93	94	**95**	96	97	98	99	100

3.

1	2	3	4	**5**	6	7	8	9	**10**
11	12	13	14	**15**	16	17	18	19	**20**
21	22	23	24	**25**	26	27	28	29	**30**
31	32	33	34	**35**	36	37	38	39	**40**
41	42	43	44	**45**	46	47	48	49	**50**
51	52	53	54	55	56	57	58	59	60
61	62	63	64	65	66	67	68	69	70
71	72	73	74	75	76	77	78	79	80
81	82	83	84	85	86	87	88	89	90
91	92	93	94	95	96	97	98	99	100

Try It

Remind students that they may use number patterns to determine what numbers are missing. Then they can check their work by counting.

Power Practice

• Have students complete the practice items. Then review each answer.

• *What is the number pattern shown by the missing numbers in item 2?* (The numbers increase by 10.)

WHAT IF THE STUDENT CAN'T

Compare Numbers

• Draw a 0–10 number line on the chalkboard. Say one of the numbers and have students name the numbers on the number line that are less than and the numbers on the number line that are greater than that number.

Complete the Power Practice

• Discuss each incorrect answer. Have students count aloud from 1 to 100 to check their responses.

Lesson Goal
- Identify place value in a two-digit number.

What the Student Needs to Know
- Count ten items.
- Identify place value.
- Read a place-value chart.

Getting Started
Display 2 tens models and 3 ones models. Ask:
- *What number do these make when I put them together?* (23)
- *How many tens are in 23?* (2) *How many ones are in 23?* (3)

Repeat, using 3 tens blocks and 2 ones blocks.

What Can I Do?
Read the question and the response. Then read and discuss the examples. Ask:
- *Why do you think tens are on the left and ones on the right in a place-value chart?* (That's the way they are arranged in a two-digit number.)
- *How would the place-value chart change to show the number 43?* (The 4 would be in the tens place, and the 3 would be in the ones place.)
- *What number is 4 tens with 3 left over?* (43)

Name_____

Place-Value Chart

Learn

Use a Place-Value Chart

This place-value chart shows tens and ones.
Tens are on the left.
Ones are on the right.

tens	ones
3	4

There are 3 tens and 4 ones in 34.

What Can I Do?
I want to write a number as tens and ones.

Rename Ones as Tens and Ones

This shows 3 tens with 4 left over.

tens	ones
3	4

Try It • Write each number in a place-value chart.

1. 59

tens	ones
5	9

2. 17

tens	ones
1	7

3. 40

tens	ones
4	0

4. 62

tens	ones
6	2

22 Grade 2, Chapter 3, Cluster A

WHAT IF THE STUDENT CAN'T

Count Ten Items
- Have the student draw a picture of 10 objects. Ask the student to count the objects aloud.

Identify Place Value
- Write a two-digit number on each of 20 cards. Have one student in a pair hold up a card and the other student say the number of tens and ones in the number. Then have students reverse roles.

Name_____

Power Practice • Write each number.

5. _52_
tens	ones
5	2

6. _37_
tens	ones
3	7

7. _11_
tens	ones
1	1

8. _75_
tens	ones
7	5

9. _48_
tens	ones
4	8

10. _66_
tens	ones
6	6

11. _90_
tens	ones
9	0

12. _14_
tens	ones
1	4

13. _23_
tens	ones
2	3

14. _82_
tens	ones
8	2

15. _9_
tens	ones
0	9

16. _45_
tens	ones
4	5

WHAT IF THE STUDENT CAN'T

Read a Place-Value Chart
• Write these numbers in a place-value chart: 28, 82, 19, 91, 46, 64. Have the student identify the number of tens and ones in each number and write the two-digit number.

Complete the Power Practice
• Discuss each incorrect answer. Have students read the number of tens and ones aloud and then say the two-digit number.
• Have students show each number with tens and ones models.

Try It
Have students say the number aloud and then state the number of tens and ones: "Fifty-nine. Five tens, nine ones."

Power Practice
• Have students write the number for each place-value chart. Discuss their answers.
• *How would item 5 change if the 2 were in the tens place and the 5 were in the ones place? (The number would be 25.)*
• *How would item 14 change if the 2 were in the tens place and the 8 were in the ones place? (The number would be 28.)*

Learn with Partners & Parents
Use a large collection of pennies (99 or fewer) to study place value.
• Dump the pennies and have children stack tens until they have made as many piles of tens as they can.
• Have children count the piles and the leftover pennies and write the two-digit number represented by the tens and ones.
• Repeat with a different number of pennies.

Lesson Goal
• Identify reasonable estimates.

What the Student Needs to Know
• Recognize the meaning of "greater" and "less."
• Count ten items.

Getting Started
Display a handful of counters. Ask:
• *How can I guess how many?* (Answers will vary.)
• *Would the number be closer to 1, 10, or 100? How do you know?* (Students may say 10, because 100 is too many and 1 is too few.)

What Can I Do?
Read the question and the response. Then read and discuss the examples. For the first example, ask:
• *How can you tell that the number of fish is closer to 10 than to 100?* (Answers will vary.)
• *How can you tell that the number of fish is less than 50?* (Answers will vary.)

For the second example, ask:
• *Is the number closer to 2 tens or to 3 tens?* (3 tens)
• *What would your estimate of the number of fish be, 20 or 30? Why?* (30, because 3 tens = 30)

Try It
Point out that the lines help students group the fish by tens. Grouping by tens is a good way to estimate in this case.

Power Practice
• Tell students to guess a number or group by tens, whichever they think will work best to solve exercises 2 and 3.

Name_____

Identify Reasonable Estimates

Learn

What Can I Do? I want to estimate how many.

Use Number Sense

Do you think there are more or fewer than 50 fish? Do you think there are more or fewer than 10 fish?

It looks like there are more than 10 and fewer than 50. A good estimate is 20 or 30 fish.

Group Tens to Estimate

You can estimate how many by grouping tens. There are nearly 3 tens, or 30 fish.

Try It • Circle the best estimate.

1. 2   (20)   200

Power Practice • Circle the best estimate.

2. 10   (30)   100

3. (10)   30   50

24 Grade 2, Chapter 3, Cluster A

© McGraw-Hill School Division

WHAT IF THE STUDENT CAN'T

Recognize the Meaning of "Greater" and "Less"
Use classroom items and people to ask questions involving greater or less.
• *Are there a greater number of boys or girls in our class?*
• *Is the number of doors in our room greater or less than the number of windows?*
• *Is the number of desks in our classroom greater or less than the number of books in our library?*

Count Ten Items
• Have students locate and count out ten items from inside their desks or cubbies.

Complete the Power Practice
• Discuss each incorrect answer. Have students show each number with hundreds, tens, and ones models. Compare numbers.

Greater Than and Less Than

Learn

Use a Number Line

Numbers on the right are greater.
Numbers on the left are less.

What Can I Do?
I want to find the greater number.

+—+
0 1 2 3 4 5 6 7 8 9 10 11 12 13 14 15 16 17 18 19 20

Think: 14 is to the left of 16.
So, 16 is greater than 14.

Compare Place Values

Look at the tens place. Which digit is greater?
If both are the same look at the ones place.
Which digit is greater?
6 is greater than 4.
So, 16 is greater than 14.

tens	ones
1	4
1	6

Try It • Use the number line.
Circle the greater number.

←—+→
0 1 2 3 4 5 6 7 8 9 10 11 12 13 14 15 16 17 18 19 20

1. (12)   2   2. 15 (17)

Power Practice • Circle the number that is greater.

3. (71) 17   4. 12 (21)   5. (33) 22

6. (68) 67   7. 50 (51)   8. 39 (40)

WHAT IF THE STUDENT CAN'T

Recognize the Meaning of "Greater" and "Less"

Ask the student questions involving greater or less.

- *Is the number of pets at your house greater or less than the number of people?*
- *Is the number of adults at your house greater or less than the number of children?*

Read a Number Line

- Draw a 0–10 number line on the chalkboard. Have the student locate and circle: 3, a number less than 3, and a number greater than 3. Then have the student do the same for the number 7.

Read a Place-Value Chart

- Write these numbers in a place-value chart: 14, 41, 29, 92, 58, 85. Have the student identify the number of tens and ones in each number and write the two-digit number.

Complete the Power Practice

- Discuss each incorrect answer. Have the student show each number with tens and ones models and compare the numbers.

USING THE LESSON

Lesson Goal

- Compare numbers to 99.

What the Student Needs to Know

- Recognize the meaning of "greater" and "less."
- Read a number line.
- Read a place-value chart.

Getting Started

On the chalkboard, draw a 0–10 number line. Ask:

- *Which number comes just after 8? (9) Which is greater, 8 or 9? (9)*
- *Which number comes just before 8? (7) Which is greater, 7 or 8? (8)*

What Can I Do?

Read the question and the response. Then read and discuss the examples. Ask:

- *If the number line continued to the right, what would the next number be? (15) Would it be greater or less than 14? (greater)*
- *The numbers 14 and 16 have the same digit in the tens place. Where do you look to figure out which number is greater? (the ones place)*

Try It

Suggest that students follow these steps:

- Find each number on the number line. Mark it.
- See which number is on the right. That number is greater.

Power Practice

- Have students complete the exercises. Discuss their answers.
- Ask: *Which strategy did you use? Was the strategy you used for item 5 the same one you used for item 6? (Answers will vary.)*

Lesson Goal
- Identify numbers that come just before, just after, and between other numbers.

What the Student Needs to Know
- Read a number line.
- Count forward 1.
- Count back 1.

Getting Started
Give five students the number cards 1–5. Have them line up in order in single file. Ask:

- *Which number comes just after 1? (2) Which number comes just before 4? (3) Which number comes between 3 and 5? (4)*

Continue with similar questions.

What Can I Do?
Read the question and the response. Then read and discuss the examples. Ask:

- *How would you find the number between two numbers on a number line?* (Point to each of the two numbers and name the number that is in between.)
- *Would you find the number that comes just before a number by counting on or counting back?* (counting back)

Try It
Students might follow these steps:
- Point to the number or numbers on the number line.
- Move to the right to find the number just after.
- Move to the left to find the number just before.
- Move to the middle to find the number between.

Power Practice
- Have the students complete the practice items. Then review each answer.

Name_____

Before, After, Between

Learn

←|—|—|—|—|—|—|—|—|—|—|—|—|—|—|—|→
0 1 2 3 4 5 6 7 8 9 10 11 12 13 14 15

What Can I Do?
I want to find the number between two numbers.

Use a Number Line

Think:
12 is just before 13.
12 is just after 11.
12 is between 11 and 13.

The numbers go in order from least to greatest.

11, 12, 13

Try It • Use the number line. Write the number.

←|—|—|—|—|—|—|—|—|—|—|—|—|—|—|—|→
0 1 2 3 4 5 6 7 8 9 10 11 12 13 14 15

1. just after 6 __7__

2. just before 10 __9__

3. between 15 and 17 __16__

Power Practice • Write the number.

4. just after 14 __15__

5. just before 18 __17__

6. just after 34 __35__

7. just before 59 __58__

8. between 76 and 78 __77__

WHAT IF THE STUDENT CAN'T

Read a Number Line
- Draw a 0–10 number line on the chalkboard. Have the student locate and circle: 5, a number less than 5, and a number greater than 5. Then ask the student to do the same for 9.

Count Forward 1
- Place counters in a line. Have the student count them. Then add one counter and have the student count again. Repeat with other numbers of counters.

Count Back 1
- Have the student count to 5 and then start at 5 and count back 1. Repeat, having the student count to 8, 14, 20, and 36, counting back 1 each time.

Complete the Power Practice
- Have the student demonstrate counting on to find the number after and counting back to find the number before.

Name_____

Skip Counting by 2s

Learn

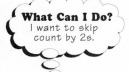

What Can I Do?
I want to skip count by 2s.

Use a Hundred Chart

Here are the first 4 rows of a hundred chart.
Start with 2 and count every other number.

1	②	3	④	5	⑥	7	⑧	9	⑩
11	⑫	13	⑭	15	⑯	17	⑱	19	⑳
21	㉒	23	㉔	25	㉖	27	㉘	29	㉚
31	㉜	33	㉞	35	㊱	37	㊳	39	㊵

Use Number Patterns

Look at the ones digits.

2 4 6 8 10 12 14 16 18 20

Use the pattern "2, 4, 6, 8, 0" to decide
what comes next.

Try It • Fill in the missing numbers.

1.

1	2	3	4	5	6	7	8	9	10
11	12	13	14	15	16	17	18	19	20
21	22	23	24	25	26	27	28	29	30
31	32	33	34	35	36	37	38	39	40
41	42	43	44	45	46	47	48	49	50

Power Practice • Write each missing number.

2. 2, 4, _6_, 8, 10, _12_

3. 32, _34_, 36, 38, 40, _42_

4. 80, 82, _84_, _86_, 88, 90

5. 66, 68, _70_, 72, _74_, 76

WHAT IF THE STUDENT CAN'T

Read a Hundred Chart

Display a hundred chart. Ask:

- *What is true of all the numbers in column 3 of the hundred chart?* (The digit in the ones place is always 3.)
- *As you move down any column, how do the numbers change?* (They increase by 10.)

Identify the Ones Digit

- Have the student choose ten numbers in the hundred chart and identify the digit in the ones place in each number.

Complete the Power Practice

- Have the student count aloud and fill in each missing number.
- Remind the student that each number he or she writes should have a 2, 4, 6, 8, or 0 in the ones place.

USING THE LESSON

Lesson Goal

- Skip count by 2s

What the Student Needs to Know

- Read a hundred chart.
- Identify the ones digit.

Getting Started

Line up ten students and give them number cards 1–10. Say:

- *Count the people.* (1, 2, 3, 4, 5, 6, 7, 8, 9, 10)

Ask every other student to step forward. Say:

- *Every other person stepped forward. What are their numbers?* (2, 4, 6, 8, 10)

What Can I Do?

Read the question and the response. Then read and discuss the examples. Ask:

- *What is true about all the numbers you count when you count by 2s?* (They all end with the digit 2, 4, 6, 8, or 0.)
- *What number comes after 20 when you count by 2s?* (22)

Try It

Some students may need to count aloud to fill in the missing numbers.

Power Practice

- Tell students to look back at the hundred chart if they have trouble.
- Ask students to check their work by looking at the ones digits in their answers.

Lesson Goal

Recognize a pattern in subtracting 2-digit numbers that have a difference of 9.

Introducing the Challenge

- On the chalkboard, write these place-value charts and have students identify the numbers represented:

tens	ones
4	3

(43)

tens	ones
3	4

(34)

Using the Challenge

- Read the directions aloud. You may want to complete the first problem as a group.
- Tell students that they may use any method they like to find each difference, such as drawing pictures or using tens and ones models.
- Discuss the pattern shown. Ask: *When did you realize that all the answers were going to be 9? Did you continue to subtract, or did you just write the answers?*

Name_____

What's the Difference?

Find the numbers shown in the place-value charts. Then subtract. What do you find?

All answers are 9.

tens	ones		tens	ones		
9	8	–	8	9	=	9

tens	ones		tens	ones		
8	7	–	7	8	=	9

tens	ones		tens	ones		
7	6	–	6	7	=	9

tens	ones		tens	ones		
6	5	–	5	6	=	9

tens	ones		tens	ones		
5	4	–	4	5	=	9

tens	ones		tens	ones		
4	3	–	3	4	=	9

tens	ones		tens	ones		
3	2	–	2	3	=	9

tens	ones		tens	ones		
2	1	–	1	2	=	9

Name_____

Counting in Portuguese

The numbers in the box are Portuguese.
They are not in order.

Read the clues.
Put the numbers in order.

Write them on a number line.

| catorze |
| doze |
| onze |
| quinze |
| treze |

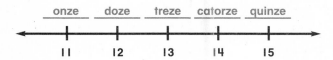

onze   doze   treze   catorze   quinze

11   12   13   14   15

Clues

1. Doze comes just before treze.

2. Catorze comes between treze and quinze.

3. Treze is greater than onze.

CHALLENGE

Lesson Goal

Use logical reasoning to determine how to count from 11 to 15 in Portuguese.

Introducing the Challenge

- Have students who speak other languages demonstrate counting to ten in that language. Explain that this worksheet will teach students how to count from 11 to 15 in Portuguese, a language spoken in Portugal, Brazil, Mozambique, Guinea-Bissau, Angola, Cape Verde, and Saõ Tome and Principe.

- You may want to point out the countries above on a map of the world.

Using the Challenge

- Read the directions aloud. Explain that by following the clues logically, students will be able to order the numbers.

- When students have completed the activity, have them share the strategies they used to order the numbers.

- Pronunciations are as follows: *own-zee, doh-zee, treh-zee, kat-or-zee, kee-zee.*

Identifying Coins

Circle the correct coin.

1. 10¢

Skip Counting by 5s and 10s

Write each missing number.

2. 5, 10, 15, 20, _____, 30, 35, _____

3. 10, 20, _____, 40, 50, _____, 70

Equal Amounts

Circle the two that show the same amount.

4.

Counting On

Write the missing number.

5. Start with _____.   I more makes _____.   I more makes _____.

Name_____

Writing Money Two Ways

Circle the two that show the same amount.

6. 20¢ $0.20 $2.00

7. $0.45 $4.50   45¢

Compare Whole Numbers

Circle the number that is greater.

8. 77   87

9. 46   45

10. 12   21

Assessment Goal

This two-page assessment covers skills identified as necessary for success in Chapter 4 Money. The first page assesses the major prerequisite skills for Cluster A. The second page assesses the major prerequisite skills for Cluster B. When the Cluster A and Cluster B prerequisite skills overlap, the skill(s) will be covered in only one section.

Getting Started

- Allow students time to look over the two pages of the assessment. Point out the labels that identify the skills covered.

- Have students find math vocabulary terms used in the assessment. List vocabulary terms on the board as students identify them. If necessary, review the meanings of all essential math vocabulary.

Introducing the Assessment

- Explain to students that these pages will help you know if they are ready to start a new chapter in their math textbooks.

- Students who have transferred from another school may not have been introduced to some of these skills. Encourage students to do their best and assure them you will help them learn any needed skills.

Cluster A Challenge

Those students who demonstrate mastery of the skills on this page will not need to use the reteaching worksheets. Instead, these students can do the Cluster A Challenge found on page 38.

Name_____

 **CHAPTER 4** What Do I Need To Know?

Identifying Coins

Circle the correct coin.

1. 10¢

Skip Counting by 5s and 10s

Write each missing number.

2. 5, 10, 15, 20, __25__, 30, 35, __40__

3. 10, 20, __30__, 40, 50, __60__, 70

Equal Amounts

Circle the two that show the same amount.

4.

Counting On

Write the missing number.

5. Start with __3__. I more makes __4__. I more makes __5__.

29A Use with Grade 2, Chapter 4, Cluster A

CLUSTER A PREREQUISITE SKILLS

The skills listed in this chart are those identified as major prerequisite skills for students' success in the lessons in Cluster A of the chapter. Each skill is covered by one or more assessment items as shown in the middle column. The right column provides the page numbers for the lessons in this book that reteach the Cluster A prerequisite skills.

Skill Name	Assessment Items	Lesson Pages
Identifying Coins	1	30
Skip Counting by 5s and 10s	2-3	31
Equal Amounts	4	32-33
Counting On	5	34

Name_____

Writing Money Two Ways

Circle the two that show the same amount.

6. (20¢)   ($0.20) $2.00

7. ($0.45) $4.50   (45¢)

Compare Whole Numbers

Circle the number that is greater.

8. 77   (87)

9. (46)   45

10. 12   (21)

CLUSTER B PREREQUISITE SKILLS

The skills listed in this chart are those identified as major prerequisite skills for students' success in the lessons in Cluster B of the chapter. Each skill is covered by one or more assessment items as shown in the middle column. The right column provides the page numbers for the lessons in this book that reteach the Cluster B prerequisite skills

Skill Name	Assessment Items	Lesson Pages
Writing Money Two Ways	6-7	35
Compare Whole Numbers	8-10	36-37

CHAPTER 4 PRE-CHAPTER ASSESSMENT

Alternative Assessment Strategies

- Oral administration of the assessment is appropriate for younger students or those whose native language is not English. Read the skills title and directions one section at a time. Check students' understanding by asking them to tell you how they will do the first exercise in the group.

- For some skill types you may wish to use group administration. In this technique, a small group or pair of students complete the assessment together. Through their discussion, you will be able to decide if supplementary reteaching materials are needed.

Intervention Materials

If students are not successful with the prerequisite skills assessed on these pages, reteaching lessons have been created to help them make the transition into the chapter.

Item correlation charts showing the skills lessons suitable for reteaching the prerequisite skills are found beneath the reproductions of each page of the assessment.

Cluster B Challenge
Those students who demonstrate mastery of the skills on this page will not need to use the reteaching worksheets. Instead, these students can do the Cluster B Challenge found on page 39.

Lesson Goal

• Identify coins: penny, nickel, dime, quarter.

What the Student Needs to Know

• Recognize the meaning of "bigger" and "smaller."

• Recognize the symbol for cents.

Getting Started

Display a pile of play coins. Ask:

• *How can I find coins that are the same?* (Look for coins that are alike in size and color.)

• *How can I find how much each coin is worth?* (Look for the number on the coin.)

What Can I Do?

Read the question and the response. Then read and discuss the examples. Ask:

• *Is the biggest coin worth the most money?* (Yes) *Is the smallest coin worth the least money?* (No) *How much is it worth?* (10¢)

• *Who is pictured on the face of the penny? the nickel? the dime? the quarter?* (Abraham Lincoln, Thomas Jefferson, Franklin Roosevelt, George Washington)

Try It

Point out that students must connect the picture of the coin to its value on the left and to its name on the right.

Power Practice

• Have students complete the practice items. Discuss their answers and how they recognized each coin.

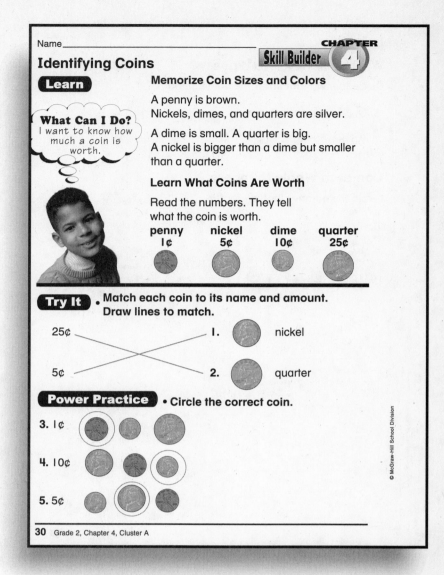

WHAT IF THE STUDENT CAN'T

Recognize the Meaning of "Bigger" and "Smaller"

• Display attribute blocks in various sizes. Have the student sort the blocks and display them in size order, from smallest to biggest.

Recognize the Symbol for Cents

• Write these amounts on the board and have students read them aloud.

5 cents 16 cents
25 cents 53 cents

• Have students rewrite each amount, using a cent sign in place of the word *cents*.

Complete the Power Practice

• Discuss each incorrect answer. Have students locate each coin from a pile of play coins.

Name_____

Skip Count by 5s and 10s

Learn

What Can I Do?
I want to skip count by 5s and 10s.

Use Number Patterns

Look at the ones digits.

5 10 15 20 25 30

10 20 30 40 50 60

Use the pattern to decide what number comes next.

Try It • Fill in the missing numbers.

1.

1	2	3	4	5	6	7	8	9	10
11	12	13	14	15	16	17	18	19	20
21	22	23	24	25	26	27	28	29	30
31	32	33	34	35	36	37	38	39	40

Power Practice • Write each missing number.

2. 25, 30, __35__, 40, 45, __50__

3. 40, __50__, 60, 70, 80, __90__

4. 50, 55, __60__, __65__, 70, 75

5. 20, 30, __40__, 50, __60__, 70

© McGraw-Hill School Division

Grade 2, Chapter 4, Cluster A **31**

WHAT IF THE STUDENT CAN'T

Read a Hundred Chart
- Display a hundred chart. Have students identify the number that is 1 more than 6 (7), 10 more than 6 (16), 1 more than 65 (66), 10 more than 65 (75), 1 more than 29 (30), 10 more than 29 (39), and so on.

Identify the Ones Digit
- Use number cards 1–99. Have the student pick ten cards. Ask him or her to identify the ones digit in each number.

Complete the Power Practice
- Make sure the student can identify whether he or she is counting by 5s or 10s in each case.
- Have the student count aloud and fill in each missing number.

USING THE LESSON

Lesson Goal
- Skip count by 5s and 10s.

What the Student Needs to Know
- Read a hundred chart.
- Identify the ones digit.

Getting Started
Display a hundred chart. Ask:
- *What is true of all the numbers in the last column of the hundred chart?* (The ones digit is 0.)
- *If you move down that column, how do the numbers change?* (They increase by 10.)

What Can I Do?
Read the question and the response. Then read and discuss the examples. Ask:
- *What is true about all the numbers you count when you count by 5s?* (The ones digit is 5 or 0.)
- *What comes after 60 when you count by 10s?* (70) *by 5s?* (65)

Try It
Counting aloud may help some students to fill in the missing numbers.

Power Practice
- Tell students to refer to the hundred chart only if they have trouble.
- Remind students to check their work by looking at the ones digits in their answers.

Lesson Goal
- Identify equivalent groups of coins.

What the Student Needs to Know
- Recognize coins.
- Skip count by 5s and 10s.
- Identify equivalencies.

Getting Started
Display a play penny, nickel, dime, and quarter. Ask:
- *Which one is worth the most?* (the quarter)
- *Which one is worth the least?* (the penny)

Have students state the value of each coin. (1¢, 5¢, 10¢, 25¢)

What Can I Do?
Read the question and the response. Then read and discuss the examples. Ask:
- *What does it mean if a coin is "worth more" than another coin?* (It has a greater value; you can buy more with it.)
- *What would the value of 3 dimes be?* (30¢) *5 dimes?* (50¢)
- *What would the value of 3 nickels be?* (15¢) *5 nickels?* (25¢)
- *What are some different ways you could use coins to make 25¢?* (1 quarter, 2 dimes and 1 nickel, 1 dime and 3 nickels, 5 nickels)

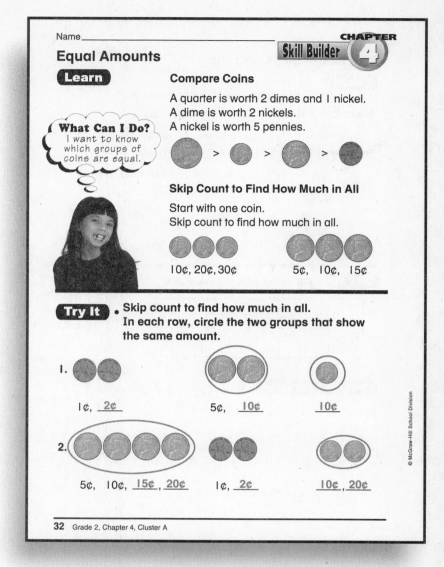

Equal Amounts

Learn

What Can I Do? I want to know which groups of coins are equal.

Compare Coins

A quarter is worth 2 dimes and 1 nickel.
A dime is worth 2 nickels.
A nickel is worth 5 pennies.

Skip Count to Find How Much in All

Start with one coin.
Skip count to find how much in all.

10¢, 20¢, 30¢   5¢, 10¢, 15¢

Try It • Skip count to find how much in all. In each row, circle the two groups that show the same amount.

1. 1¢, _2¢_   5¢, _10¢_   _10¢_

2. 5¢, 10¢, _15¢_, _20¢_   1¢, _2¢_   _10¢_, _20¢_

© McGraw-Hill School Division

WHAT IF THE STUDENT CAN'T

Recognize Coins
- Display a play penny, nickel, dime, and quarter. Have the student arrange them from least value to greatest value.
- Display a play penny, nickel, dime, and quarter. Remove one and have the student tell which coin is missing and what its value is.

Skip Count by 5s and 10s
- Give the student a pile of 5 play nickels and a pile of 5 play dimes. Have them use skip counting to find the total value of each pile.
- Give the student a hundred chart and have the student use it to count by 5s and 10s to 100.

Power Practice

Circle the two that show the same amount.

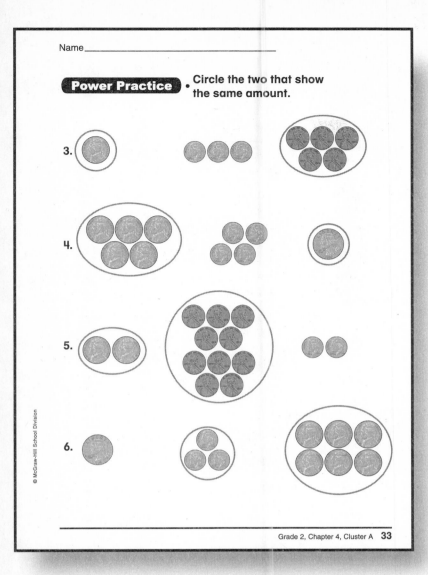

3.

4.

5.

6.

© McGraw-Hill School Division

USING THE LESSON

Try It

Remind students that in order to know what number to skip count by, they must identify the value of the coins pictured. A nickel, for example, indicates that they must skip count by 5s.

Power Practice

- Have students complete the practice items. Discuss their answers.
- Have volunteers write the value of the equivalent groups of coins using a cent sign. (5¢, 25¢, 10¢, 30¢)
- *How else might you show 10¢?* (1 nickel, 5 pennies; 1 dime.)

Learn with Partners & Parents

Use a pile of mixed coins to practice forming equivalent groups.

- First have students sort the coins into groups of the same kinds of coins.
- Then ask them to use the coins to show at least two ways to make 10¢, 20¢, 25¢, 40¢, and 50¢.

WHAT IF THE STUDENT CAN'T

Identify Equivalencies

- Write these facts and sums on the chalkboard and have students match the equivalencies.

  2 + 2   5 + 5   10 + 10
    10   20   4

  Repeat with similar examples.

Complete the Power Practice

- Discuss each incorrect answer. Have students identify the value of each group of coins pictured.

USING THE LESSON

Lesson Goal
- Count on by 1s.

What the Student Needs to Know
- Read a number line.
- Count by 1s.
- Draw a given number of objects.

Getting Started
Give students this problem:
- *Jenny is 7. How old will she be on her next birthday? (8) How old will she be on the birthday after that? (9) How old will she be on the birthday after that? (10)*

What Can I Do?
Read the question and the response. Then read and discuss the examples. Ask:
- *Start at 4 on the number line. Go up 1. Then go up 1 more. Where are you? (6)*
- *Start by drawing 4 objects. Draw 1 more. Then draw 1 more. How many objects have you drawn? (6 objects)*

Try It
Students might follow these steps:
- Point to the number on the number line.
- Move to the right to find 1 more.
- Write the number.

Power Practice
- Have students complete the practice items. Then review each answer.

Name_____

Counting On

Skill Builder — CHAPTER 4

Learn

What Can I Do? I want to count on to find how many in all.

Use a Number Line

Each number goes up by one.
Move up one to count on one.

```
0 1 2 3 4 5 6 7 8 9 10
```

4 and one more is 5 and one more is 6.

Draw a Picture

Draw the number you have.
Draw 1 more. Count.
Draw 1 more. Count.

○○○○   ⦻⦻

Try It • Use the number line.
Find 1 more.

```
0 1 2 3 4 5 6 7 8 9 10
```

1. 3 and 1 more = __4__   2. 6 and 1 more = __7__

3. 1 and 1 more = __2__   4. 8 and 1 more = __9__

Power Practice • Write each missing number.

5. Start with 5. 1 more makes __6__. 1 more makes __7__.

6. Start with 3. 1 more makes __4__. 1 more makes __5__.

7. Start with 7. 1 more makes __8__.
   1 more makes __9__. 1 more makes __10__.

© McGraw-Hill School Division

34 Grade 2, Chapter 4, Cluster A

WHAT IF THE STUDENT CAN'T

Read a Number Line
- Draw a 0–10 number line on the chalkboard. Have the student locate and circle: 5, the number that is 1 more than 5 (6); 7, the number that is 1 more than 7 (8).

Count by 1s
- Line up 5 counters. Have the student count them. Add 1 more. Have the student tell how many there are now. If necessary, the student may count the whole group. Repeat with different numbers of counters until the student does not need to return to 1 to count on.

Draw a Given Number of Objects
- Have the student practice by having them draw 3 flowers, 4 flowerpots, 5 trees, 6 rabbits, and so on. Have the student count the number of objects aloud.

Complete the Power Practice
- Have the student count on with counters to model items 5–7.

Name_____

Writing Money Two Ways

Skill Builder   **CHAPTER 4**

Learn

What Can I Do?
I want to write money amounts with dollar signs or cents signs.

Read $ and ¢ Symbols

The symbol ¢ is read "cents." Read 32¢ as "thirty-two cents."

The symbol $ means "dollars." Read $1.32 as "one dollar and thirty-two cents." Numbers before the decimal point are dollars. Numbers after the decimal point are cents.

Look at Place Value

A decimal point separates dollars from cents.

dollars		dimes	pennies
$1	.	3	2

Try It • Do the numbers show the same amount? Circle yes or no.

1. $0.60   60¢   (yes)   no   **2.** $2.50   25¢   yes   (no)

3. $0.43   34¢   yes   (no)   **4.** $0.95   95¢   (yes)   no

Power Practice • Circle the two that show the same amount.

5. $1.24   (24¢)   ($0.24)   **6.** (68¢)   ($0.68) $6.80

7. (53¢) $5.53   ($0.53)   **8.** ($0.35)   (35¢) $3.05

9. $1.66   (66¢)   ($0.66)   **10.** $99.00   ($0.99)   (99¢)

© McGraw-Hill School Division

Grade 2, Chapter 4, Cluster B **35**

WHAT IF THE STUDENT CAN'T

Recognize Dollar and Cent Signs

- Write these dollars-and-cents amounts on the board and have students read them aloud:

  $1.00 $2.40 $5.93

- Have students rewrite these phrases, using a cent sign in place of the word *cents*.

  15 cents   38 cents   99 cents

Read a Place-Value Chart

- Write these numbers in a place-value chart: 123, 410, 708, 999. Have the student identify the number of hundreds, tens, and ones in each number and write the three-digit number.

Complete the Power Practice

- Discuss each incorrect answer. Have the student read each amount aloud.

Lesson Goal

- Use dollar and cent signs.

What the Student Needs to Know

- Recognize dollar and cent signs.
- Read a place-value chart.

Getting Started

- Display a play dollar, a play dime, and a play penny. Write these amounts on the chalkboard and have students identify the play money that matches each one: $0.01, $0.10, $1.00.

What Can I Do?

Read the question and the response. Then read and discuss the examples. Ask:

- *How many pennies are equal to 1 dime?* (10) *How many pennies are equal to 1 dollar?* (100)
- *Write these amounts on the chalkboard and have students read them aloud: $0.42, $4.20, $0.39, $3.90.* (forty-two cents, four dollars and twenty cents, thirty-nine cents, three dollars and ninety cents)

Try It

Students might read each pair of amounts aloud to see whether they are equivalent.

Power Practice

- Have students complete the exercises. Discuss their answers.
- Ask: *How can place value help you figure out which two amounts are the same?* (Knowing that the decimal point divides dollars from cents helps you read the amounts.)

Lesson Goal
- Compare numbers to 99.

What the Student Needs to Know
- Recognize the meaning of "greater" and "less."
- Read a number line.
- Read a place-value chart.

Getting Started
Have students count aloud from 0 to 20. Ask:
- *Which numbers are greater than 10? (11, 12, . . . 20)*

What Can I Do?
Read the question and the response. Then read and discuss the example. Ask:
- *Which number is to the right of 15? (16)*
- *Which number is greater? (16)*
- *Which number is to the left of 18? (17)*
- *Which number is less? (17)*
- *How can you use place value to compare the numbers 16 and 17?* (Look at the tens digits. Since they are the same, look at the ones digits. 7 ones is greater than 6 ones, so 17 is greater than 16.)

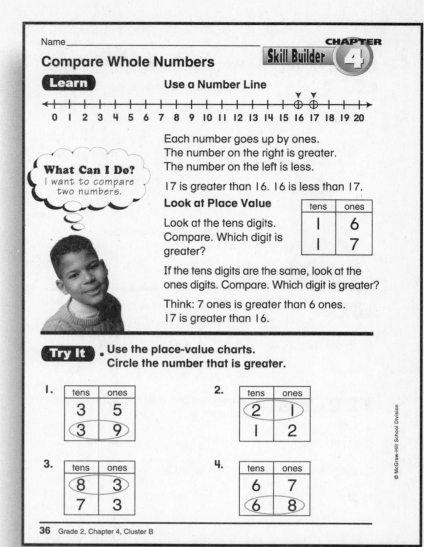

Name_____

Compare Whole Numbers

Learn   Use a Number Line

0 1 2 3 4 5 6 7 8 9 10 11 12 13 14 15 16 17 18 19 20

What Can I Do? I want to compare two numbers.

Each number goes up by ones.
The number on the right is greater.
The number on the left is less.

17 is greater than 16. 16 is less than 17.

Look at Place Value

tens	ones
1	6
1	7

Look at the tens digits. Compare. Which digit is greater?

If the tens digits are the same, look at the ones digits. Compare. Which digit is greater?

Think: 7 ones is greater than 6 ones. 17 is greater than 16.

Try It   Use the place-value charts. Circle the number that is greater.

1.
tens	ones
3	5
3	9

2.
tens	ones
2	1
1	2

3.
tens	ones
8	3
7	3

4.
tens	ones
6	7
6	8

36 Grade 2, Chapter 4, Cluster B

© McGraw-Hill School Division

WHAT IF THE STUDENT CAN'T

Recognize the Meaning of "Greater" and "Less"
- Give a student a pile of counters. Have the student separate the pile into two groups, count each group of counters, and tell which number is greater and which is less.

Read a Number Line
Draw a 0–10 number line on the chalkboard. Ask:
- *Which number is the greatest? (10)*
- *Which number is the least? (0)*
- *Which numbers are greater than 5? (6, 7, 8, 9, 10)*
- *Which numbers are less than 5? (0, 1, 2, 3, 4)*

Name_____

Power Practice • Circle the number that is greater.

5. 68 (86)

6. (24) 23

7. 19 (91)

8. 39 (40)

9. (27) 25

10. (61) 60

11. (13) 11

12. (55) 45

13. (98) 89

14. 67 (77)

15. (56) 50

16. (75) 57

17. 22 (33)

18. (90) 9

19. (86) 68

20. (49) 48

© McGraw-Hill School Division

Grade 2, Chapter 4, Cluster B **37**

WHAT IF THE STUDENT CAN'T

Read a Place-Value Chart
• Write these numbers in a place-value chart: 18, 81, 45, 54, 27, 72. Have the student identify the number of tens and ones in each number and write the two-digit number.

Complete the Power Practice
• Discuss each incorrect answer. Have students identify the number of tens and ones in each number, compare tens, and then compare ones.

USING THE LESSON

Try It
Remind students to compare tens before comparing ones. If the tens digits differ, they do not need to look at the ones.

Power Practice
• Have students complete the practice items. Then review each answer. Discuss the strategies students used to find the greater number.

Grade 2, Chapter 4, Cluster B **37**

CHALLENGE

Lesson Goal
Find one or more groups of coins that have the same value as a given group.

Introducing the Challenge
- Give each pair of students a pile of play coins. Have them demonstrate the following:
- *Show two ways to make 8¢.* (8 pennies, 1 nickel and 3 pennies)
- *Show four ways to make 12¢.* (1 dime and 2 pennies, 1 nickel and 7 pennies, 2 nickels and 2 pennies, 12 pennies)

Using the Challenge
- Read the directions aloud. If necessary, students may use play money to model the problems.
- After students complete the activity, have them suggest other ways to make the amounts shown. (For example, 24¢ might be 1 dime, 2 nickels, and 4 pennies; 18¢ might be 1 dime, 1 nickel, and 3 pennies; 32¢ might be 1 quarter and 7 pennies, and so on.)

Two Ways to Pay

The coins show one way to pay.
Think of another way.
Write the missing numbers.

24¢

Another way to pay: __4__ nickels, 4 pennies

18¢

Another way to pay: __3__ nickels, 3 pennies

32¢

Another way to pay: __1__ quarter, __1__ nickel, __2__ pennies

45¢

Another way to pay: __4__ dimes, __1__ nickel

Another way to pay: __9__ nickels

Another way to pay: 3 dimes, __3__ nickels

© McGraw-Hill School Division

A Maze of Money

Make the coins add up to the amount at the bottom.
Pick one from the top row, one from the middle row,
and one from the bottom row.
Use each coin or group of coins only once.
Draw lines. The first one is done for you.

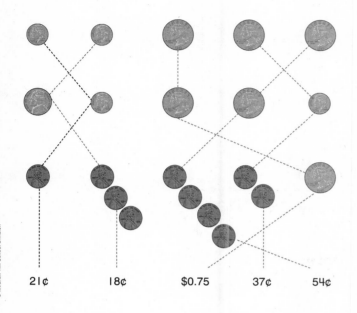

21¢   18¢ $0.75   37¢   54¢

© McGraw-Hill School Division

CHALLENGE

Lesson Goal

Find a group of coins that has a value that matches a given value.

Introducing the Challenge

- Give pairs of students a pile of play coins. Challenge them to make these amounts using only three coins: 16¢, 27¢, 40¢, 51¢. (1 dime, 1 nickel, and 1 penny; 1 quarter and 2 pennies; 1 quarter, 1 dime, and 1 nickel; 2 quarters and 1 penny)

Using the Challenge

- Read the directions aloud. Point out that although there are many ways to solve some of the items, they are to use each coin or group of coins only once.

- When students have completed the activity, have them find other ways to make some of the amounts shown with the coins given.

Addition Facts to 20

Add.

1.

tens	ones
	9
+	7

2.

tens	ones
	5
+	3

Place Value

Write each number in a place-value chart.

3. 64

tens	ones

4. 29

tens	ones

Renaming Ones as Tens and Ones

Write each number two ways.

5.

_____ ones

_____ ten _____ one

6.

_____ ones

_____ tens _____ ones

Turnaround Facts

Add.

7. 8 + 5 = _____

5 + 8 = _____

8. 3 + 7 = _____

7 + 3 = _____

Round to the Nearest Ten

Use the number line.
Round each number to the nearest ten.

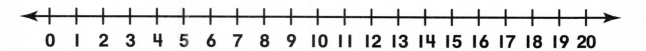

0 1 2 3 4 5 6 7 8 9 10 11 12 13 14 15 16 17 18 19 20

9. 18 _____

10. 12 _____

Assessment Goal

This two-page assessment covers skills identified as necessary for success in Chapter 5 Add 2-Digit Numbers. The first page assesses the major prerequisite skills for Cluster A. The second page assesses the major prerequisite skills for Cluster B. When the Cluster A and Cluster B prerequisite skills overlap, the skill(s) will be covered in only one section.

Getting Started

- Allow students time to look over the two pages of the assessment. Point out the labels that identify the skills covered.
- Have students find math vocabulary terms used in the assessment. List vocabulary terms on the board as students identify them. If necessary, review the meanings of all essential math vocabulary.

Introducing the Assessment

- Explain to students that these pages will help you know if they are ready to start a new chapter in their math textbooks.
- Students who have transferred from another school may not have been introduced to some of these skills. Encourage students to do their best and assure them you will help them learn any needed skills.

Cluster A Challenge

Those students who demonstrate mastery of the skills on this page will not need to use the reteaching worksheets. Instead, these students can do the Cluster A Challenge found on page 48.

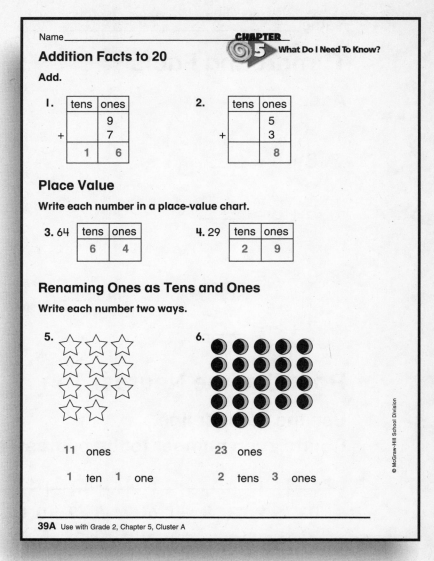

Name_____

Addition Facts to 20

Add.

1.
tens	ones
	9
+	7
1	6

2.
tens	ones
	5
+	3
	8

Place Value

Write each number in a place-value chart.

3. 64
tens	ones
6	4

4. 29
tens	ones
2	9

Renaming Ones as Tens and Ones

Write each number two ways.

5.

11 ones

1 ten 1 one

6.

23 ones

2 tens 3 ones

© McGraw-Hill School Division

39A Use with Grade 2, Chapter 5, Cluster A

CLUSTER A PREREQUISITE SKILLS

The skills listed in this chart are those identified as major prerequisite skills for students' success in the lessons in Cluster A of the chapter. Each skill is covered by one or more assessment items as shown in the middle column. The right column provides the page numbers for the lessons in this book that reteach the Cluster A prerequisite skills.

Skill Name	Assessment Items	Lesson Pages
Addition Facts to 20	1-2	40
Place Value	3-4	41
Renaming Ones as Tens and Ones	5-6	42-43

Name_____

Turnaround Facts

Add.

7. $8 + 5 =$ ___13___

$5 + 8 =$ ___13___

8. $3 + 7 =$ ___10___

$7 + 3 =$ ___10___

Round to the Nearest Ten

Use the number line.
Round each number to the nearest ten.

```
◄─┼─┼─┼─┼─┼─┼─┼─┼─┼─┼─┼─┼─┼─┼─┼─┼─┼─┼─┼─┼─►
  0 1 2 3 4 5 6 7 8 9 10 11 12 13 14 15 16 17 18 19 20
```

9. 18 ___20___

10. 12 ___10___

CLUSTER B PREREQUISITE SKILLS

The skills listed in this chart are those identified as major prerequisite skills for students' success in the lessons in Cluster B of the chapter. Each skill is covered by one or more assessment items as shown in the middle column. The right column provides the page numbers for the lessons in this book that reteach the Cluster B prerequisite skills

Skill Name	Assessment Items	Lesson Pages
Turn-Around Facts	7-8	44-45
Round to the Nearest Ten	9-10	46-47

Alternative Assessment Strategies

- Oral administration of the assessment is appropriate for younger students or those whose native language is not English. Read the skills title and directions one section at a time. Check students' understanding by asking them to tell you how they will do the first exercise in the group.

- For some skill types you may wish to use group administration. In this technique, a small group or pair of students complete the assessment together. Through their discussion, you will be able to decide if supplementary reteaching materials are needed.

Intervention Materials

If students are not successful with the prerequisite skills assessed on these pages, reteaching lessons have been created to help them make the transition into the chapter.

Item correlation charts showing the skills lessons suitable for reteaching the prerequisite skills are found beneath the reproductions of each page of the assessment.

Cluster B Challenge

Those students who demonstrate mastery of the skills on this page will not need to use the reteaching worksheets. Instead, these students can do the Cluster B Challenge found on page 49.

Lesson Goal
- Add facts to 20.

What the Student Needs to Know
- Add doubles.
- Add or subtract one.
- Read a place-value chart.

Getting Started
Give each pair of students 10 counters. Ask:
- *How many ways can you arrange the counters in 2 groups?*

Have volunteers write the resulting groups as number sentences.

(1 + 9 = 10, 2 + 8 = 10, 3 + 7 = 10, . . . 9 + 1 = 10)

What Can I Do?
Read the question and the response. Then read and discuss the examples. Ask:
- *How does knowing that 6 + 6 = 12 help you know the answer to 6 + 7?* (Because 7 is 1 more than 6, the answer will be 1 more than 12, or 13.)
- *How does knowing that 8 + 8 = 16 help you know the answer to 8 + 7?* (Because 7 is 1 less than 8, the answer will be 1 less than 16, or 15.)

Try It
You may wish to have students describe the relationship between the sentences in each pair before finding the sums.

Power Practice
- Ask students to think about place value to make sure they align numbers correctly as they add.
- Have students complete the practice items. Then review each answer.

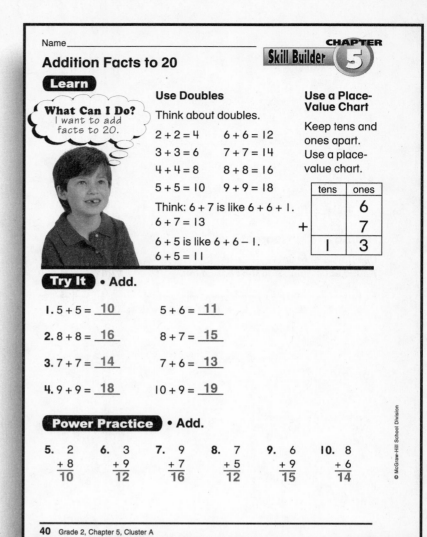

WHAT IF THE STUDENT CAN'T

Add Doubles
- Make flash cards with doubles from 1 + 1 to 6 + 6. Have students work in pairs to practice adding doubles.

Add or Subtract One
- Line up 9 counters. Have the student count them. Add 1 more. Have the student state the result as a number sentence ("9 plus 1 equals 10.") Take away 1 counter and have the student state the result. ("10 minus 1 equals 9.") Repeat with other numbers of counters.

Read a Place-Value Chart
- Write these numbers in a place-value chart: 87, 42, 19, 63. Have the student identify the number of tens and ones in each number and write the 2-digit number.

Complete the Power Practice
- Discuss each incorrect answer. Have the student model any fact he or she missed using counters.

Place Value

Learn

What Can I Do?
I want to know the number of tens and ones in a number.

Use a Place-Value Chart

Write the number 34 in a place-value chart.

tens	ones
3	4

34 has 3 tens and 4 ones.

Understanding Place Value

The ones digit is on the right. The tens digit is to the left of the ones digit.

The 4 tells how many ones are in 34.
The 3 tells how many tens are in 34.

Try It • Write each number in a place-value chart.

1. 78

tens	ones
7	8

2. 39

tens	ones
3	9

3. 14

tens	ones
1	4

4. 60

tens	ones
6	0

Power Practice • Write the number of tens and ones.

5. 82 __8__ tens __2__ ones   6. 47 __4__ tens __7__ ones

7. 24 __2__ tens __4__ ones   8. 90 __9__ tens __0__ ones

9. 55 __5__ tens __5__ ones   10. 18 __1__ ten __8__ ones

Grade 2, Chapter 5, Cluster A **41**

WHAT IF THE STUDENT CAN'T

Read a Place-Value Chart
- Play Place-Value Bingo with students. Instead of calling out a number such as "38," call out "3 tens and 8 ones," and have students mark the appropriate number. Continue to play the game in this manner until someone has Bingo.

Distinguish Left from Right
- Write the digits 0–9 on large cards. Mix them and have the student pick two cards to make a two-digit number. Have the student place his or her hands on the cards and tell which digit is on the left (tens digit) and which is on the right (ones digit). Then

have the student say the number. Continue with other numbers.

Complete the Power Practice
- Discuss each incorrect answer. Have students show each number with tens and ones models.

USING THE LESSON

Lesson Goal
- Identify place value in 2-digit numbers.

What the Student Needs to Know
- Read a place-value chart.
- Distinguish left from right.

Getting Started
Draw a place-value chart on the chalkboard. Ask:
- *Which column shows the tens?* (the left column) *Which column shows the ones?* (the right column)
- *How would you write the number 56 in the chart?* (5 on the left, 6 on the right)

What Can I Do?
Read the question and the response. Then read and discuss the examples. Ask:
- *In the number 34, what does the 4 stand for?* (4 ones) *What does the 3 stand for?* (3 tens)
- *How do you know that 34 is the same as 30 + 4?* (34 is 3 tens, or 30, plus 4 ones)

Try It
To prepare students for addition of 2-digit numbers, suggest that they write the ones first and the tens next.

Power Practice
- Have students complete the practice items. Discuss their answers.
- Point out that 8 tens 2 ones is the same as 80 + 2; 4 tens 7 ones is the same as 40 + 7, and so on.

Lesson Goal
• Rename ones as tens and ones.

What the Student Needs to Know
• Identify place value.
• Count ten items.

Getting Started
• Display a hundred chart. Have each student select a number to read aloud and then state the number of tens and ones in the number chosen.
• *What happens to the tens as you read down a column of the chart?* (They go up by 1 ten.)
• *What happens to the ones as you read down a column of the chart?* (They remain the same.)

What Can I Do?
Read the question and the response. Then read and discuss the examples. Ask:
• *How many tens and ones are there in 15 ones?* (1 ten, 5 ones) *23 ones?* (2 tens 3 ones) *20 ones?* (2 tens, 0 ones)
• *Does it matter which items you circle when you circle tens?* (No.)

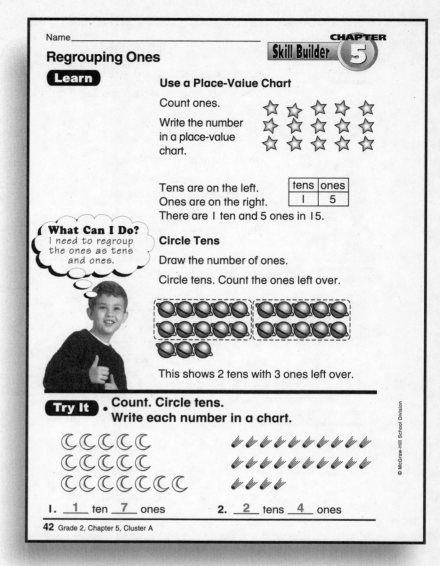

What If The Student Can't

Identify Place Value
• Write 2-digit numbers on the chalkboard and have the student identify the number of tens and ones in each number.

• Provide tens and ones models and have the student use them to show a variety of two-digit numbers.

Name_____

Power Practice • Write each number two ways.

☆☆☆☆☆
☆☆☆☆☆
☆☆☆☆☆

3. __16__ ones
   __1__ ten __6__ ones

✎✎✎✎✎✎✎✎✎✎
✎✎✎✎✎✎✎✎✎✎
✎✎✎✎✎✎✎✎✎✎

4. __30__ ones
   __3__ tens __0__ ones

☾☾☾☾☾☾☾☾☾☾
☾☾☾☾☾☾☾☾☾☾
☾☾

5. __22__ ones
   __2__ tens __2__ ones

◯◯◯◯◯◯◯◯◯◯
◯◯◯◯◯◯◯◯◯◯
◯◯◯◯◯◯◯◯◯◯
◯◯◯◯◯

6. __35__ ones
   __3__ tens __5__ ones

✎✎✎✎✎✎✎✎✎✎
✎✎✎✎✎✎✎✎✎✎
✎✎✎✎✎✎✎✎✎✎
✎✎✎✎✎✎✎✎✎✎

7. __41__ ones
   __4__ tens __1__ one

☾☾☾☾☾☾☾☾☾☾
☾☾☾☾☾☾☾☾☾

8. __19__ ones
   __1__ ten __9__ ones

◯◯◯◯◯
◯◯◯◯◯
◯◯◯◯

9. __14__ ones
   __1__ ten __4__ ones

☆☆☆☆☆☆☆☆☆☆
☆☆☆☆☆☆☆☆☆☆
☆☆☆☆☆☆☆☆

10. __28__ ones
    __2__ tens __8__ ones

Try It

Be sure students understand that they should count each group of 10, circle each group of 10, and write the number in the place-value chart.

Power Practice

- Point out that students may circle groups of ten if it helps them find the number of tens and ones.
- Have students complete the practice items. Then review each answer.

WHAT IF THE STUDENT CAN'T

Count Ten Items

- Place fifteen counters in random order. Have the student count out ten. Repeat using 12, 16, and 19 counters.

Complete the Power Practice

- Discuss each incorrect answer. Have volunteers read their answers aloud as equations; for example, "16 ones equals 1 ten, 6 ones."

Lesson Goal

- Use the Commutative Property of Addition.

What the Student Needs to Know

- Draw a picture to match a number sentence.
- Recall addition facts to 20.

Getting Started

On a felt board, display a group of 7 shapes and a group of 6 shapes. Ask:

- *Would I add or subtract to find how many in all?* (add)

Write: 7 + 6 = 13

Flip the felt board so that the group of 6 shapes is on the left. Ask:

- *Would I add or subtract to find how many in all?* (add)

Write: 6 + 7 = ? Ask:

- *What is the sum? How do you know?* (13; it will be the same as 7 + 6.)

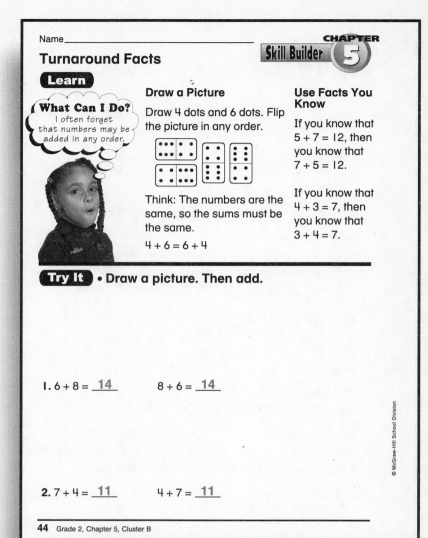

Name_____

CHAPTER 5
Skill Builder

Turnaround Facts

Learn

What Can I Do?
I often forget that numbers may be added in any order.

Draw a Picture

Draw 4 dots and 6 dots. Flip the picture in any order.

Think: The numbers are the same, so the sums must be the same.

4 + 6 = 6 + 4

Use Facts You Know

If you know that 5 + 7 = 12, then you know that 7 + 5 = 12.

If you know that 4 + 3 = 7, then you know that 3 + 4 = 7.

Try It • Draw a picture. Then add.

1. 6 + 8 = __14__   8 + 6 = __14__

2. 7 + 4 = __11__   4 + 7 = __11__

44 Grade 2, Chapter 5, Cluster B

© McGraw-Hill School Division

WHAT IF THE STUDENT CAN'T

Draw a Picture to Match a Number Sentence

- Supply counters and ask students to model a given addition fact to 20. Then have them draw or trace the counters, flip the picture, and give both number sentences; for example, 4 + 6 = 10 and 6 + 4 = 10.
- Ask students to work with a partner or in small groups to draw pictures to illustrate some of the addition facts to 20.

Recall Addition Facts to 20

- Make up flash cards with addition facts to 20 and have pairs of students quiz each other.
- Have students work in teams in an "Addition Facts Bee." Line up two teams and give the first player in Team 1 a fact to solve. If he or she solves it correctly, that team goes again. If not, the fact goes to Team 2. Continue until everyone has had two chances to find a sum.

Name_____

3. $5 + 8 = \underline{13}$

$8 + 5 = \underline{13}$

4. $7 + 6 = \underline{13}$

$6 + 7 = \underline{13}$

5. $9 + 7 = \underline{16}$

$7 + 9 = \underline{16}$

6. $4 + 9 = \underline{13}$

$9 + 4 = \underline{13}$

7. $3 + 6 = \underline{9}$

$6 + 3 = \underline{9}$

8. $8 + 4 = \underline{12}$

$4 + 8 = \underline{12}$

9. $3 + 9 = \underline{12}$

$9 + 3 = \underline{12}$

10. $7 + 8 = \underline{15}$

$8 + 7 = \underline{15}$

USING THE LESSON

What Can I Do?

Read the question and the response. Then read and discuss the examples. Ask:

- *What can dominoes teach you about addition facts?* (They can show you that the sum is the same no matter how you order the addends.)

- *If you know that 4 + 6 = 10, what other addition fact do you know?* (6 + 4 = 10)

- *If you know that 7 + 5 = 12, what other addition fact do you know?* (5 + 7 = 12)

Try It

Tell students that they may choose any object to draw for their addition pictures. Discuss their answers.

Power Practice

- Suggest that students complete the facts they know first, and use those facts to find the sums they don't immediately know.

- Have students complete the practice items. Then review their answers.

WHAT IF THE STUDENT CAN'T

Complete the Power Practice

- Provide paper and pencil and have students draw pictures for the facts they missed.

- If students found two different sums for the facts in a pair, provide counters and have them model the facts.

Lesson Goal
- Round numbers to the nearest ten.

What the Student Needs to Know
- Count by tens.
- Read a number line.
- Identify the ones digit.

Getting Started
- Have students count by 10s to 100.
- Display a hundred chart and have students locate the 10s. (10, 20, 30, . . . 100)

What Can I Do?
Read the question and the response. Then read and discuss the examples. Ask:

- *What does it mean when you say "18 rounds up to 20"?* (20 is the nearest ten to 18, and it is greater, so you have to round up.)
- *What does it mean when you say "32 rounds down to 30"?* (30 is the nearest ten to 32, and it is less, so you have to round down.)
- *Would you round 55 up or down? Why?* (Up; you round up when the ones digit is 5 or greater.)

Name_____

Round to the Nearest Ten

Learn

Use a Number Line

What Can I Do?
I want to round a number to the nearest ten.

The number 18 is between 10 and 20. It is closer to 20. So 18 rounds up to 20.

10 11 12 13 14 15 16 17 18 19 20

The number 32 is between 30 and 40. It is closer to 30. So 32 rounds down to 30.

30 31 32 33 34 35 36 37 38 39 40

Use the Ones Digit

If the ones digit is less than 5, round down. If it is 5 or greater, round up.
Round 64 down to 60. Round 65 up to 70.

Try It • Use the number line. Round to the nearest ten.

1. 51 __50__   50 51 52 53 54 55 56 57 58 59 60

2. 17 __20__   10 11 12 13 14 15 16 17 18 19 20

3. 34 __30__   30 31 32 33 34 35 36 37 38 39 40

© McGraw-Hill School Division

WHAT IF THE STUDENT CAN'T

Count by Tens
- Give the student 10 play dimes and have the student count by tens to 1 dollar.
- Have the student use tens models to show the tens from 10 to 100. Then have the student count the models by tens.

Read a Number Line
- Draw a 0–10 number line on the chalkboard. Have students locate a number you say, the number that is 1 less, and the number that is 1 greater.

Name_____

Power Practice • Look at the ones digit. Round each number to the nearest ten.

4. 81 __80__   5. 24 __20__   6. 38 __40__

7. 62 __60__   8. 33 __30__   9. 74 __70__

10. 45 __50__   11. 13 __10__   12. 9 __10__

13. 78 __80__   14. 65 __70__   15. 44 __40__

16. 26 __30__   17. 77 __80__   18. 88 __90__

Grade 2, Chapter 5, Cluster B **47**

WHAT IF THE STUDENT CAN'T

Identify the Ones Digit
- Have students practice identifying the ones digit by writing the numbers in items 4-18 in place-value charts.

Complete the Power Practice
- Review the rules for rounding: round down if the ones digit is 0–4; round up if the ones digit is 5–9.
- Have students circle the ones digit before rounding the number.

Try It
Suggest that students use these steps:
- Find the number on the number line.
- Find the tens on either side of that number.
- Decide which ten is closer to the number.
- Write that ten.

Power Practice
- If students have trouble, they might draw a number line to help them.
- Have students complete the practice items. Then review each answer.

Learn with Partners & Parents
Have students use the ages of people in their families to practice rounding to the nearest ten.
- Give each student a hundred chart to take home.
- Have students circle numbers on the hundred chart that represent family members' ages.
- Tell students to round each family member's age to the nearest ten and write a sentence for each person; for example, *To the nearest ten, Grandpa Dennis is 70. To the nearest ten, I am 10.*

CHALLENGE

Lesson Goal
Find pairs of addends that have a sum of 100.

Introducing the Challenge
Draw a 0–10 number line on the chalkboard. Say:

- *Find two numbers that add up to 10. Circle them.*

Repeat until students have circled a variety of number pairs.

Using the Challenge
- Read the directions aloud. Explain that students should use a different color for each of the ten pairs of numbers they find.

- Discuss ways in which one might use the hundred chart to add. Point out that if students circle, for example, 88, that they can count the number of squares that have numbers greater than 88 to find the other addend, 12.

Make 100

Find two numbers that add up to 100.
Color them red.

Find two more.
Color them blue.

Continue until you have colored 10 pairs of numbers.
Share your number sentences with the class.

1	2	3	4	5	6	7	8	9	10
11	12	13	14	15	16	17	18	19	20
21	22	23	24	25	26	27	28	29	30
31	32	33	34	35	36	37	38	39	40
41	42	43	44	45	46	47	48	49	50
51	52	53	54	55	56	57	58	59	60
61	62	63	64	65	66	67	68	69	70
71	72	73	74	75	76	77	78	79	80
81	82	83	84	85	86	87	88	89	90
91	92	93	94	95	96	97	98	99	100

Possible answers include 1 + 99, 2 + 98, 3 + 97, . . ., 41 + 49.

1. _____ + _____ = 100

2. _____ + _____ = 100

3. _____ + _____ = 100

4. _____ + _____ = 100

5. _____ + _____ = 100

6. _____ + _____ = 100

7. _____ + _____ = 100

8. _____ + _____ = 100

9. _____ + _____ = 100

10. _____ + _____ = 100

Name_____

Order of Addition

**Draw pictures.
Then add.**

$8 + 9 =$ __17__ $9 + 8 =$ __17__

$5 + 7 =$ __12__ $7 + 5 =$ __12__

**Use what you learned.
Add.**

$15 + 12 = 27$ $12 + 15 =$ __27__

$24 + 42 = 66$ $42 + 24 =$ __66__

$38 + 19 = 57$ $19 + 38 =$ __57__

$384 + 6 = 390$ $6 + 384 =$ __390__

$444 + 138 = 582$ $138 + 444 =$ __582__

CHALLENGE

Lesson Goal

Use the Commutative Property of Addition to find the sum of 2- or 3-digit numbers.

Introducing the Challenge

Give each student 12 counters. Say:

- *Form two different-sized groups with the counters. Say the two addition sentences the groups show.*

- Have students share their answers with the class.

Using the Challenge

Read the directions aloud. Have a volunteer state the rule they learned in "Turn-Around Facts." (Numbers may be added in any order; the sum is the same.)

- Have students complete the activity independently.

Subtraction Facts

Subtract.

1.

tens	ones
1	3
−	5

2.

tens	ones
	7
−	3

Place Value

Write each number in a place-value chart.

3. 46

tens	ones

4. 98

tens	ones

Renaming Tens and Ones

Write each number two ways.

5.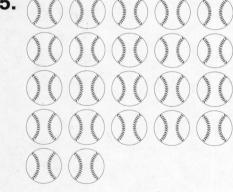

_____ tens _____ ones

_____ ones

6.

_____ ten _____ ones

_____ ones

Name _____

Fact Families

Complete each fact family.

7. 9 + 3 = _____

3 + 9 = _____

12 − 9 = _____

12 − 3 = _____

8. 1 + 7 = _____

7 + 1 = _____

8 − 1 = _____

8 − 7 = _____

Round to the Nearest Ten

Use the number line.
Round each number to the nearest ten.

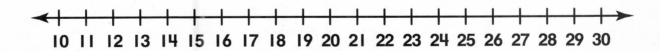

10 11 12 13 14 15 16 17 18 19 20 21 22 23 24 25 26 27 28 29 30

9. 13 _____

10. 29 _____

Assessment Goal

This two-page assessment covers skills identified as necessary for success in Chapter 6 Subtract 2-Digit Numbers. The first page assesses the major prerequisite skills for Cluster A. The second page assesses the major prerequisite skills for Cluster B. When the Cluster A and Cluster B prerequisite skills overlap, the skill(s) will be covered in only one section.

Getting Started

- Allow students time to look over the two pages of the assessment. Point out the labels that identify the skills covered.
- Have students find math vocabulary terms used in the assessment. List vocabulary terms on the board as students identify them. If necessary, review the meanings of all essential math vocabulary.

Introducing the Assessment

- Explain to students that these pages will help you know if they are ready to start a new chapter in their math textbooks.
- Students who have transferred from another school may not have been introduced to some of these skills. Encourage students to do their best and assure them you will help them learn any needed skills.

Cluster A Challenge

Those students who demonstrate mastery of the skills on this page will not need to use the reteaching worksheets. Instead, these students can do the Cluster A Challenge found on page 56.

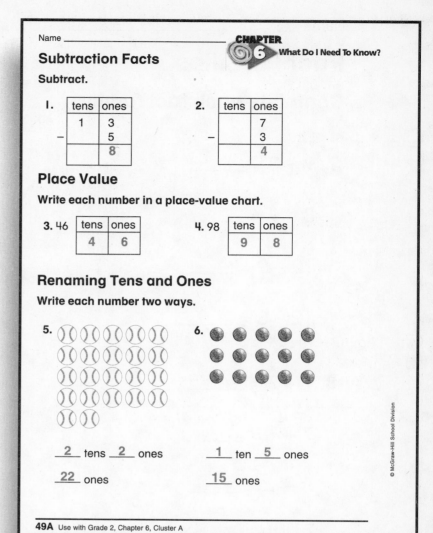

Name _____

CHAPTER 6 What Do I Need To Know?

Subtraction Facts

Subtract.

1.
tens	ones
1	3
−	5
	8

2.
tens	ones
	7
−	3
	4

Place Value

Write each number in a place-value chart.

3. 46
tens	ones
4	6

4. 98
tens	ones
9	8

Renaming Tens and Ones

Write each number two ways.

5.

__2__ tens __2__ ones

__22__ ones

6.

__1__ ten __5__ ones

__15__ ones

© McGraw-Hill School Division

49A Use with Grade 2, Chapter 6, Cluster A

CLUSTER A PREREQUISITE SKILLS

The skills listed in this chart are those identified as major prerequisite skills for students' success in the lessons in Cluster A of the chapter. Each skill is covered by one or more assessment items as shown in the middle column. The right column provides the page numbers for the lessons in this book that reteach the Cluster A prerequisite skills.

Skill Name	Assessment Items	Lesson Pages
Subtraction Facts to 20	1-2	50
Place Value	3-4	51
Renaming Tens and Ones	5-6	52-53

Name _____

Fact Families

Complete each fact family.

7. $9 + 3 = \underline{12}$

$3 + 9 = \underline{12}$

$12 - 9 = \underline{3}$

$12 - 3 = \underline{9}$

8. $1 + 7 = \underline{8}$

$7 + 1 = \underline{8}$

$8 - 1 = \underline{7}$

$8 - 7 = \underline{1}$

Round to the Nearest Ten

Use the number line.
Round each number to the nearest ten.

10 11 12 13 14 15 16 17 18 19 20 21 22 23 24 25 26 27 28 29 30

9. 13 $\underline{10}$

10. 29 $\underline{30}$

Alternative Assessment Strategies

- Oral administration of the assessment is appropriate for younger students or those whose native language is not English. Read the skills title and directions one section at a time. Check students' understanding by asking them to tell you how they will do the first exercise in the group.

- For some skill types you may wish to use group administration. In this technique, a small group or pair of students complete the assessment together. Through their discussion, you will be able to decide if supplementary reteaching materials are needed.

Intervention Materials

If students are not successful with the prerequisite skills assessed on these pages, reteaching lessons have been created to help them make the transition into the chapter.

Item correlation charts showing the skills lessons suitable for reteaching the prerequisite skills are found beneath the reproductions of each page of the assessment.

CLUSTER B PREREQUISITE SKILLS

The skills listed in this chart are those identified as major prerequisite skills for students' success in the lessons in Cluster B of the chapter. Each skill is covered by one or more assessment items as shown in the middle column. The right column provides the page numbers for the lessons in this book that reteach the Cluster B prerequisite skills

Skill Name	Assessment Items	Lesson Pages
Fact Families	7-8	54
Round to the Nearest Ten	9-10	55

Cluster B Challenge

Those students who demonstrate mastery of the skills on this page will not need to use the reteaching worksheets. Instead, these students can do the Cluster B Challenge found on page 57.

Lesson Goal
• Subtract facts to 20.

What the Student Needs to Know
• Add doubles.
• Recognize the inverse relation-ship between addition and subtraction.
• Read a place-value chart.

Getting Started
Give each pair of students 10 counters. Say:

• *How many different ways can you take away counters from 10?*

Have volunteers write the resulting groups as number sentences.
(10 – 1 = 9, 10 – 2 = 8,
10 – 3 = 7, . . .10 – 9 = 1)

What Can I Do?
Read the question and the response. Then read and discuss the examples. Ask:

• *How does knowing 5 + 5 = 10 help you know 10 – 5 = 5?* (Because subtracting 5 from 10 is the opposite of adding 5 + 5.)

• *Why is it important to line up the digits when you subtract?* (So that tens and ones are clearly shown and understood.)

Try It
You may wish to have students describe the relationship between the sentences in each pair before finding the differences.

Power Practice
• Ask students to think about place value to make sure they align numbers correctly as they subtract.
• Have students complete the practice items. Then review each answer.

Name_____

Subtraction Facts to 20

Learn

What Can I Do? I want to subtract facts to 20.

Use Doubles
Think about doubles:
$5 + 5 = 10$ and $10 - 5 = 5$.

You can use doubles to find $11 - 6$.

Think: 11 is 1 more than 10.
$11 - 5$ is 1 more than $10 - 5$.
So, $11 - 5 = 6$.

Use a Place-Value Chart
A place-value chart helps you keep the tens and ones apart.

	tens	ones
	1	5
–		7
		8

Try It • Subtract.

1. $16 - 8 = \underline{8}$

   $17 - 8 = \underline{9}$

2. $14 - 7 = \underline{7}$

   $15 - 7 = \underline{8}$

3. $8 - 4 = \underline{4}$

   $9 - 4 = \underline{5}$

4. $12 - 6 = \underline{6}$

   $13 - 6 = \underline{7}$

Power Practice • Subtract.

5. 12	6. 13	7. 16	8. 13	9. 14	10. 17
-8	-9	-7	-5	-8	-9
4	4	9	8	6	8

WHAT IF THE STUDENT CAN'T

Add Doubles
• Have the student use doubles flash cards to practice doubles addition from 1 + 1 to 9 + 9. Ask the student to model each double addition with connecting cubes.

Recognize the Inverse Relationship Between Addition and Subtraction
• Give the student a variety of subtraction doubles facts and have them check their answers using addition.

Read a Place-Value Chart
• Write these numbers in a place-value chart: 45, 31, 27, 90. Have the student identify the number of tens and ones in each number and write the two-digit number.

Complete the Power Practice
• Discuss each incorrect answer. Have the student model any fact he or she missed using counters.

Place Value

CHAPTER **Skill Builder 6**

Learn

What Can I Do?
I want to know the number of tens and ones in a number.

Use a Place-Value Chart

Write the number 78 in a chart.

tens	ones
7	8

78 has 7 tens and 8 ones.

Use Expanded Notation

$78 = 70 + 8$
$70 = 7$ tens
 $8 = 8$ ones

$78 = 7$ tens 8 ones

Try It • Write each number in a place-value chart.

1. 45

tens	ones
4	5

2. 37

tens	ones
3	7

3. 23

tens	ones
2	3

4. 50

tens	ones
5	0

Power Practice • Write the number of tens and ones.

5. 61 __6__ tens __1__ one

6. 19 __1__ ten __9__ ones

7. 88 __8__ tens __8__ ones

8. 70 __7__ tens __0__ ones

9. 94 __9__ tens __4__ ones

10. 12 __1__ ten __2__ ones

© McGraw-Hill School Division

Grade 2, Chapter 6, Cluster A **51**

WHAT IF THE STUDENT CAN'T

Read a Place-Value Chart
• Give the student tens and ones models and have them show these numbers: 15, 28, 34. Then have them use their models to write the numbers in a place-value chart.

Complete the Power Practice
• Discuss each incorrect answer. Have students show each number with tens and ones models.

Lesson Goal
• Identify place value in 2-digit numbers.

What the Student Needs to Know
• Read a place-value chart.

Getting Started
• Give pairs of students a handful of place-value models. Have them show the following numbers and tell how many tens and ones are in each: 34, 50, 76, 92. (3 tens 4 ones, 5 tens 0 ones, 7 tens 6 ones, 9 tens 2 ones)

What Can I Do?
Read the question and the response. Then read and discuss the examples. Ask:
• *In the number 78, what does the 8 mean?* (8 ones) *What does the 7 mean?* (7 tens)
• *How can you use expanded notation to prove that 78 is the same as 7 tens 8 ones?* ($78 = 70 + 8$. $70 = 7$ tens. $8 = 8$ ones.)

Try It
To prepare students for subtraction of 2-digit numbers, suggest that they write the ones first and the tens last.

Power Practice
• Have students complete the practice items. Discuss their answers.
• Point out that 6 tens 1 one is the same as $60 + 1$; 1 ten 9 ones is the same as $10 + 9$, and so on.

Lesson Goal
• Rename tens and ones as ones.

What the Student Needs to Know
• Identify place value.
• Count ten items.
• Identify coins.

Getting Started
• Distribute tens and ones models to small groups of students. Have students pick one tens model and show the number of ones that are equal to 1 ten. (10 ones) Continue with 1 ten 2 ones (12 ones), 2 tens 3 ones (23 ones), 1 ten 8 ones (18 ones), and so on.

What Can I Do?
Read the question and the response. Then read and discuss the examples. Ask:

• *How many ones are there in 4 tens and 2 ones? (42 ones) 6 tens and 8 ones? (68 ones) 3 tens and 0 ones? (30 ones)*

• *How many pennies would you have if you traded 2 dimes and 5 pennies for pennies? (25 pennies)*

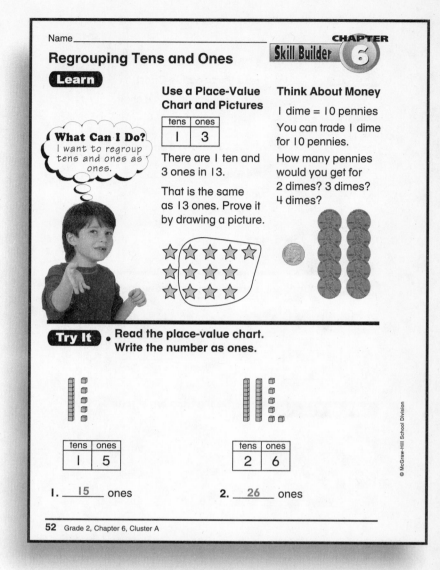

Name_____

Regrouping Tens and Ones

Learn

What Can I Do? I want to regroup tens and ones as ones.

Use a Place-Value Chart and Pictures

tens	ones
1	3

There are 1 ten and 3 ones in 13.

That is the same as 13 ones. Prove it by drawing a picture.

Think About Money

1 dime = 10 pennies

You can trade 1 dime for 10 pennies.

How many pennies would you get for 2 dimes? 3 dimes? 4 dimes?

Try It • Read the place-value chart. • Write the number as ones.

tens	ones
1	5

1. ___15___ ones

tens	ones
2	6

2. ___26___ ones

52 Grade 2, Chapter 6, Cluster A

© McGraw-Hill School Division

WHAT IF THE STUDENT CAN'T

Identify Place Value
• Give students a hundred chart. Have them choose five numbers at random and tell the number of tens and ones in each number.

Count Ten Items
• Give pairs of students tens and ones models. Have them take turns counting out 10 ones and trading them for 1 ten.

Name_____

Power Practice • Write each number two ways.

3. __1__ ten __4__ ones

__14__ ones

4. __5__ tens __0__ ones

__50__ ones

5. __3__ tens __1__ one

__31__ ones

6. __2__ tens __2__ ones

__22__ ones

7. __4__ tens __3__ ones

__43__ ones

8. __1__ tens __8__ ones

__18__ ones

© McGraw-Hill School Division

USING THE LESSON

Try It

If students have difficulty, remind them that they may draw a picture to help them find the number of ones.

Power Practice

- Have students complete the practice items. Then review each answer. Ask:
- *Which number in items 3–8 is greatest?* (50) *Which number is least?* (14)

Learn with Partners & Parents

Students can practice renaming by using dimes and pennies.

- Give the child a pile of pennies and a pile of dimes. Offer suggestions such as the following:
- *Show the number of pennies you could trade for 1 dime, 2 dimes, 3 dimes.* (10, 20, 30)
- *Show the number of dimes you could trade for 10 pennies, 20 pennies, 30 pennies.* (1, 2, 3)

WHAT IF THE STUDENT CAN'T

Identify Coins

- Have students repeat the exercise entitled "Count Ten Items" using dimes and pennies instead of tens and ones models.
- Give the student a pile of play coins and have the student sort the coins into piles of pennies, nickels, dimes, and quarters. Then have the student tell what each coin is worth.

Complete the Power Practice

- Discuss each incorrect answer. Have volunteers read their answers aloud as equations; for example, "1 ten 4 ones equals 14 ones."

Lesson Goal
- Complete a family of addition and subtraction facts.

What the Student Needs to Know
- Write a number sentence.
- Use the Commutative Property of Addition.
- Recall addition and subtraction facts to 20.

Getting Started
On a felt board, display a group of 5 shapes and a group of 8 shapes. Ask:

- *If I asked how many shapes there are in all, what number sentence would you write?* (5 + 8 = 13)

Flip the felt board. Ask:

- *What number sentence describes this picture now?* (8 + 5 = 13)

Take away 5 shapes. Ask:

- *What number sentence would describe what I just did?* (13 − 5 = 8)

Replace the 5 shapes. Take away 8 shapes. Ask:

- *What number sentence would describe what I just did?* (13 − 8 = 5)

What Can I Do?
Read the question and the response. Then read and discuss the examples. Ask:

- *When you add two numbers, which is the greatest number in an addition sentence?* (the last number; the sum)
- *When you subtract one number from another, which is the greatest number in a subtraction sentence?* (the first number)

Try It
Remind students that a fact family contains only three numbers, and the numbers are the same from fact to fact. Discuss their answers.

Power Practice
- Have students complete the practice items. Then review their answers.

Name _____

Fact Families

Learn

What Can I Do?
I can't remember all four facts in a fact family.

Write Number Sentences
Begin with an addition fact, such as 7 + 8 = 15. Put the numbers together in different addition and subtraction sentences.

7 + 8 = 15	8 + 7 = 15
15 − 8 = 7	15 − 7 = 8

The 2 addition sentences and 2 subtraction sentences make a fact family.

Use Facts You Know
If you know that 7 + 8 = 15, then you know that 8 + 7 = 15. Numbers may be added in any order.

Try It • Complete each fact family.

1. 6 + 8 = __14__
   8 + 6 = __14__
   14 − 8 = __6__
   14 − 6 = __8__

2. 7 + 3 = __10__
   3 + 7 = __10__
   10 − 3 = __7__
   10 − 7 = __3__

Power Practice • Use the numbers. Write the fact family.

3. 5, 7, 12
   __5 + 7 = 12__
   __7 + 5 = 12__
   __12 − 7 = 5__
   __12 − 5 = 7__

4. 7, 9, 16
   __7 + 9 = 16__
   __9 + 7 = 16__
   __16 − 9 = 7__
   __16 − 7 = 9__

WHAT IF THE STUDENT CAN'T

Write a Number Sentence
- Display two groups of counters and have the student write the two related addition sentences. Take away one group and have the student write the related subtraction sentence. Then take away the other group and have the student write the other related subtraction sentence.

Use the Commutative Property of Addition
- Give the student dominoes and have the student say and write the two addition sentences represented by each one.

Recall Addition and Subtraction Facts to 20
- Make up flash cards with addition and subtraction facts to 20 and have pairs of students quiz each other and model each fact with counters.

Complete the Power Practice
- Provide paper and pencil and have students draw pictures for the facts they missed.
- Remind students that all four facts in a family contain the same three numbers.

Name_____

Round to the Nearest Ten

Learn

What Can I Do?
I want to round a number to the nearest ten.

Use a Number Line

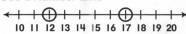
10 11 12 13 14 15 16 17 18 19 20

12 is between 10 and 20. It is closer to 10. So, 12 rounds down to 10.

17 is between 10 and 20. It is closer to 20. So 17 rounds up to 20.

Use the Ones Digit

If the ones digit is less than 5, round down. Round 14 down to 10.

If the ones digit is 5 or greater, round up. Round 15 up to 20.

Try It • **Use the number line. Round to the nearest ten.**

1. 31 ___30___   ←+++++++++++→
30 31 32 33 34 35 36 37 38 39 40

2. 58 ___60___   ←+++++++++++→
50 51 52 53 54 55 56 57 58 59 60

Power Practice • **Look at the ones digit. Round each number to the nearest ten.**

3. 73 ___70___   4. 19 ___20___   5. 25 ___30___

6. 54 ___50___   7. 36 ___40___   8. 88 ___90___

9. 42 ___40___   10. 65 ___70___   11. 7 ___10___

Grade 2, Chapter 6, Cluster B **55**

WHAT IF THE STUDENT CAN'T

Count by Tens
• Have the student use tens models to show tens from 10 to 100. Then have the student count the models by tens.

Read a Number Line
• Draw a 70–80 number line on the chalkboard. Have students locate a number you say and name the ten to the left (70) and the ten to the right (80).

Identify the Ones Digit
• Students may practice identifying the ones digit by writing the numbers in items 3-11 in place-value charts.

Complete the Power Practice
• Review the rules for rounding: down if the ones digit is 0–4, up if the ones digit is 5–9.

USING THE LESSON

Lesson Goal
• Round numbers to the nearest ten.

What the Student Needs to Know
• Count by tens.
• Read a number line.
• Identify the ones digit.

Getting Started
Have students count by 10s to 100. Ask:
• *How many tens are in 40?* (4) *How many tens are in 70?* (7)

What Can I Do?
Read the question and the response. Then read and discuss the examples. Ask:
• *What does it mean when you say "17 rounds up to 20"?* (20 is the nearest ten to 17, and it is greater, so you have to round up.)
• *What does it mean when you say "12 rounds down to 10"?* (10 is the nearest ten to 12, and it is less, so you have to round down.)
• *Would you round 35 up or down? Why?* (Up; you round up when the ones digit is 5 or greater.)

Try It
Suggest that students find the number on the number line first and then look at the tens to the left and the right to determine which is closer.

Power Practice
• Have students complete the practice items. Then review each answer.

Lesson Goal

Identify subtraction sentences that have a difference of 15.

Introducing The Challenge

- Challenge students to suggest subtraction sentences that have a difference of 15. Write them on the chalkboard as they are mentioned.

Using The Challenge

- Read the directions aloud. Explain that students should only color those puzzle pieces that contain a sentence with a difference of 15.

- Remind students that they may check subtraction by adding; for example 20 − 5 = 15; 15 + 5 = 20.

- *How can you tell just by looking that 30 − 16 will not have a difference of 15? (Subtracting the ones shows that the ones digit in the difference will be 4, not 5.)*

- *How can you tell just by looking that 90 − 45 will not have a difference of 15? (9 tens are far more than 4 tens, so the answer will be more than 15.)*

Name_____

A Difference of 15

Color only the subtraction sentences with a difference of 15.

What do you see?

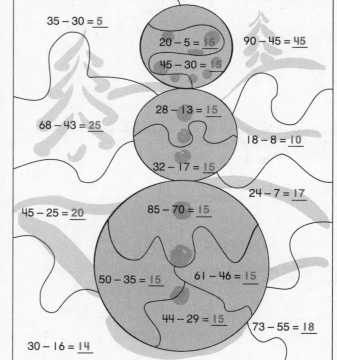

$35 - 30 = \underline{5}$

$20 - 5 = \underline{15}$

$45 - 30 = \underline{15}$

$90 - 45 = \underline{45}$

$68 - 43 = \underline{25}$

$28 - 13 = \underline{15}$

$18 - 8 = \underline{10}$

$32 - 17 = \underline{15}$

$24 - 7 = \underline{17}$

$45 - 25 = \underline{20}$

$85 - 70 = \underline{15}$

$50 - 35 = \underline{15}$

$61 - 46 = \underline{15}$

$44 - 29 = \underline{15}$

$73 - 55 = \underline{18}$

$30 - 16 = \underline{14}$

Name_____

Math of Planet X

**Fact families on Planet X are the same as on Earth.
Numbers are different.**

Here are some facts from Planet X.
Complete each fact family.

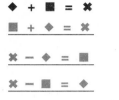

◆ + ■ = ✖

■ + ◆ = ✖

✖ − ◆ = ■

✖ − ■ = ◆

★ − ➤ = ♥

★ − ♥ = ➤

➤ + ♥ = ★

♥ + ➤ = ★

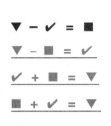
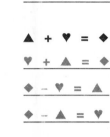

▼ − ✔ = ■

▼ − ■ = ✔

✔ + ■ = ▼

■ + ✔ = ▼

▲ + ♥ = ◆

♥ + ▲ = ◆

◆ − ♥ = ▲

◆ − ▲ = ♥

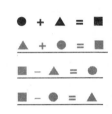

● + ▲ = ■

▲ + ● = ■

■ − ▲ = ●

■ − ● = ▲

Lesson Goal

Use non-numerical symbols to form families of statements that have the structure of addition and subtraction fact families.

Introducing The Challenge

- Have students complete this fact family: 7 + 8 = 15. (8 + 7 = 15, 15 − 7 = 8, 15 − 8 = 7)

- *What is true about the four facts in a fact family?* (All four facts use the same three numbers; two are addition facts, and two are subtraction facts.)

Using The Challenge

- Read the directions aloud.

- Have a volunteer "read" the first number sentence aloud. ("Diamond plus square equals X.") Ask:

- *What is the greatest "number" in this fact family?* (X) *How do you know?* (It is the sum of the other two numbers.)

- Have students complete the activity independently.

Time to the Hour

Write the time.

1.

2.

_____   _____

Time to the Half Hour

Write the time.

3.

4.

_____   _____

Skip Count by 5s

Fill in the missing numbers.

5. 5, 10, _____, 20, _____, 30, 35, _____

Ordinal Numbers

Follow the directions.

6. Draw a circle around the third animal.

7. Make an X on the sixth animal.

8. Draw a hat on the fourth animal.

9. Give the ninth animal a flag.

10. Draw a star on the second animal.

CHAPTER 7 PRE-CHAPTER ASSESSMENT

Assessment Goal

This two-page assessment covers skills identified as necessary for success in Chapter 7 Time. The first page assesses the major prerequisite skills for Cluster A. The second page assesses the major prerequisite skills for Cluster B. When the Cluster A and Cluster B prerequisite skills overlap, the skill(s) will be covered in only one section.

Getting Started

- Allow students time to look over the two pages of the assessment. Point out the labels that identify the skills covered.
- Have students find math vocabulary terms used in the assessment. List vocabulary terms on the board as students identify them. If necessary, review the meanings of all essential math vocabulary.

Introducing the Assessment

- Explain to students that these pages will help you know if they are ready to start a new chapter in their math textbooks.
- Students who have transferred from another school may not have been introduced to some of these skills. Encourage students to do their best and assure them you will help them learn any needed skills.

Cluster A Challenge

Those students who demonstrate mastery of the skills on this page will not need to use the reteaching worksheets. Instead, these students can do the Cluster A Challenge found on page 62.

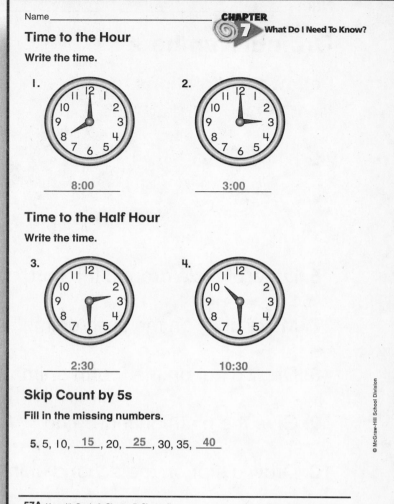

Name_____

Time to the Hour

Write the time.

1. 8:00

2. 3:00

Time to the Half Hour

Write the time.

3. 2:30

4. 10:30

Skip Count by 5s

Fill in the missing numbers.

5. 5, 10, __15__, 20, __25__, 30, 35, __40__

© McGraw-Hill School Division

57A Use with Grade 2, Chapter 7, Cluster A

CLUSTER A PREREQUISITE SKILLS

The skills listed in this chart are those identified as major prerequisite skills for students' success in the lessons in Cluster A of the chapter. Each skill is covered by one or more assessment items as shown in the middle column. The right column provides the page numbers for the lessons in this book that reteach the Cluster A prerequisite skills.

Skill Name	Assessment Items	Lesson Pages
Time to the Hour	1-2	58
Time to the Half Hour	3-4	59
Skip Count by 5s	5	60

Name_____

Ordinal Numbers

Follow the directions.

6. Draw a circle around the third animal.

7. Make an X on the sixth animal.

8. Draw a hat on the fourth animal.

9. Give the ninth animal a flag.

10. Draw a star on the second animal.

© McGraw-Hill School Division

Use with Grade 2, Chapter 7, Cluster B **57B**

Alternative Assessment Strategies

• Oral administration of the assessment is appropriate for younger students or those whose native language is not English. Read the skills title and directions one section at a time. Check students' understanding by asking them to tell you how they will do the first exercise in the group.

• For some skill types you may wish to use group administration. In this technique, a small group or pair of students complete the assessment together. Through their discussion, you will be able to decide if supplementary reteaching materials are needed.

Intervention Materials

If students are not successful with the prerequisite skills assessed on these pages, reteaching lessons have been created to help them make the transition into the chapter.

Item correlation charts showing the skills lessons suitable for reteaching the prerequisite skills are found beneath the reproductions of each page of the assessment.

CLUSTER B PREREQUISITE SKILLS

The skills listed in this chart are those identified as major prerequisite skills for students' success in the lessons in Cluster B of the chapter. Each skill is covered by one or more assessment items as shown in the middle column. The right column provides the page numbers for the lessons in this book that reteach the Cluster B prerequisite skills

Skill Name	Assessment Items	Lesson Pages
Ordinal Numbers	6-10	61

Cluster B Challenge

Those students who demonstrate mastery of the skills on this page will not need to use the reteaching worksheets. Instead, these students can do the Cluster B Challenge found on page 63.

Lesson Goal

• Tell time to the hour.

What the Student Needs to Know

• Identify hour and minute hands.

Getting Started

Set a play clock for 9:00. Ask:

• *Where is the big hand?* (on the 12) *Where is the small hand?* (on the 9) *What time is it?* (9 o'clock)

Repeat with other times to the hour.

What Can I Do?

Read the question and the response. Then read and discuss the examples. Ask:

• *Which hand shows the hours?* (the small hand)

• *Which hand shows the minutes?* (the big hand)

• *What are two ways to write the same time?* (the number followed by o'clock and with 2 dots after the number)

Try It

Point out to students that when time is written with two dots in the middle (:), the hour comes before the dots, and the minutes come after the dots. In these exercises, the dots are provided.

Power Practice

• Explain that for these exercises, students should write both the time using the dots and numbers and "o'clock."

• Have students complete the practice items. Then review each answer.

WHAT IF THE STUDENT CAN'T

Identify Hour and Minute Hands

• Give the student a play clock. Ask the student to set the hour hand to 10 and the minute hand to 12 and tell the time. Continue with other times.

Ask questions like this:

• *If the big hand is on the 12 and the small hand is on the 5, what time is it?* (5 o'clock)

Complete the Power Practice

• Have the student read the time shown on the clock aloud before writing it using a colon.

• Remind students that the hour comes before the dots, and the minutes come after the dots.

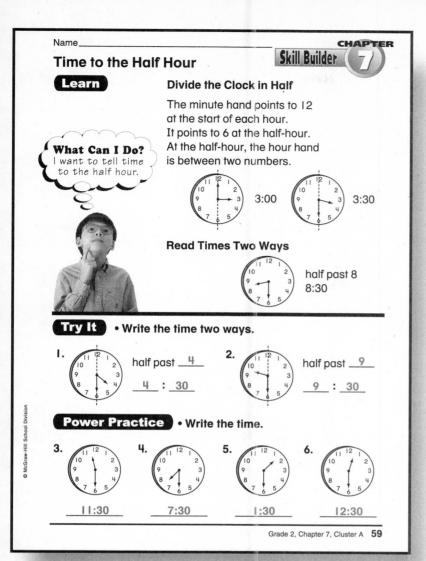

Name_____

Time to the Half Hour

Skill Builder

Learn

What Can I Do?
I want to tell time to the half hour.

Divide the Clock in Half

The minute hand points to 12 at the start of each hour.
It points to 6 at the half-hour.
At the half-hour, the hour hand is between two numbers.

3:00   3:30

Read Times Two Ways

half past 8
8:30

Try It • Write the time two ways.

1. half past _4_
    _4_ : _30_

2. half past _9_
    _9_ : _30_

Power Practice • Write the time.

3. _11:30_

4. _7:30_

5. _1:30_

6. _12:30_

© McGraw-Hill School Division

WHAT IF THE STUDENT CAN'T

Identify Hour and Minute Hands

- Give the student a play clock. Have the student set the hour hand to 8 and the minute hand to 12 and tell the time. Continue with other times to the hour and half hour.

Recognize One-Half

- Give the student a paper plate and a crayon or marker. Ask the student to draw a line on the plate to divide it in half.

Read Times

- Use digital form to write times to the hour and half hour on index cards. Have the student pick a card and read the time aloud, and show the time on the play clock. Repeat.

Complete the Power Practice

- Have the student read the time shown aloud before writing it using a colon.
- Remind students that when a clock shows half past, the hour hand is between numbers. The number that names the hour is the lesser number.

USING THE LESSON

Lesson Goal

- Tell time to the half hour.

What the Student Needs to Know

- Identify hour and minute hands.
- Recognize one-half.
- Read times.

Getting Started

Set a play clock at 2:00. Ask:

- *What time is it?* (2 o'clock)

Move the minute hand clockwise to 6 and the hour hand between 2 and 3. Ask:

- *Where is the minute hand?* (on 6) *Where is the hour hand?* (between 2 and 3) *What time is it now?* (2:30)

What Can I Do?

Read the question and the response. Then read and discuss the examples. Ask:

- *How many minutes go by between 3 o'clock and 3:30?* (30)
- *Why do we call 8:30 "half past eight"?* (It is halfway between 8 and 9 or half past 8 o'clock.)

Try It

Remind students that the hour comes before the dots and the minutes come after the dots. In these exercises, the dots are provided.

Power Practice

- Have students complete the practice items.

Learn with Partners & Parents

Have students play Clock Concentration.

- Use digital form to write times to the hour and half hour on index cards. On another set of cards write those same times using "o'clock" or "half past."
- Players mix up all the cards and place them facedown.
- Players take turns finding pairs of matching times.

Lesson Goal
• Skip count by 5s.

What the Student Needs to Know
• Read a hundred chart.
• Identify the ones digit.

Getting Started
Show students how to count fives on their fingers. Display the fingers of one hand one at a time and count:

• *1, 2, 3, 4, 5.*

Write 5 on the chalkboard. Begin again, counting:

• *6, 7, 8, 9, 10.*

Write 10 on the chalkboard. Have students imitate you as you continue to count from 15 through 50.

What Can I Do?
Read the question and the response. Then read and discuss the examples. Ask:

• *What is true about all the numbers you count when you count by 5s?* (The ones digit is 5 or 0.)
• *What comes after 50 when you count by 5s?* (55) *What comes after 85 when you count by 5s?* (90)

Try It
Some students may need to count aloud to fill in the missing numbers.

Power Practice
• Have students complete the practice items. Tell them to look back at the hundred chart if they have trouble.

Name_____

Skip Count by 5s

Learn

What Can I Do?
I want to skip count by 5s.

Use a Hundred Chart
The chart shows the numbers from 1 to 100. Look at the pattern for 5s.

1	2	3	4	5	6	7	8	9	10
11	12	13	14	15	16	17	18	19	20
21	22	23	24	25	26	27	28	29	30
31	32	33	34	35	36	37	38	39	40
41	42	43	44	45	46	47	48	49	50
51	22	53	54	55	56	57	58	59	60
61	62	63	64	65	66	67	68	69	70
71	72	73	74	75	76	77	78	79	80
81	82	83	84	85	86	87	88	89	90
91	92	93	94	95	96	97	98	99	100

Use Number Patterns
Look at the ones digits.

5, 10, 15, 20, 25, 30

Use the pattern "5, 0, 5, 0, 5, 0" to decide what number comes next.

Try It • Fill in the missing numbers.

1.

21	22	23	24	25	26	27	28	29	30
31	32	33	34	35	36	37	38	39	40
41	42	43	44	45	46	47	48	49	50

Power Practice • Write each missing number.

2. 15, 20, __25__, 30, 35, __40__

3. 30, __35__, 40, 45, 50, __55__

4. 10, 15, __20__, __25__, 30, 35

© McGraw-Hill School Division

WHAT IF THE STUDENT CAN'T

Read a Hundred Chart
• Display a hundred chart. Have the student identify all the numbers that contain 5 ones (5, 15, 25,. . . 95) and all the numbers that contain 0 ones (10, 20, 30,. . .100). Circle all these numbers on the chart and ask the student to count with you by 5s to 100.

Identify the Ones Digit
• Have the student choose ten numbers in the hundred chart and identify the digit in the ones place in each number.

Complete the Power Practice
• Have the student count aloud and fill in each missing number. Watch for students who need to return to 5 each time; they may need additional practice.
• Remind the student that each number he or she writes should have a 5 or 0 in the ones place.

Name_____

Ordinal Numbers

CHAPTER 7
Skill Builder

Learn

What Can I Do?
I want to use numbers to put things in order.

Use Numbers to Count and to Order

Use the top numbers to count things.
Use the bottom numbers to put things in order.

one	two	three	four	five	six	seven	eight	nine	ten
first	second	third	fourth	fifth	sixth	seventh	eighth	ninth	tenth

Count from 1 to 10. Put things in order from first to tenth.

Try It • Draw lines to match.

1. two   2. five   3. seven

fifth   seventh   second

Power Practice • Follow the directions.

brown   yellow   red   orange

4. Color the third duckling yellow.

5. Color the tenth duckling orange.

6. Color the sixth duckling red.

7. Color the first duckling brown.

Grade 2, Chapter 7, Cluster B **61**

WHAT IF THE STUDENT CAN'T

Count to Ten
- Provide the student with a pile of counters. Have the student count off ten.
- Ask the student to write the numbers on a blank 0–10 number line.

Complete the Power Practice
Suggest that students follow these steps:
- Find the ordinal number in the direction.
- Match the ordinal number to a counting number. For example, for *third*, think *three*.
- Count from left to right. Color the duckling the correct color.

USING THE LESSON

Lesson Goal
- Identify the position of objects using ordinal numbers.

What the Student Needs to Know
- Count to ten.

Getting Started
Give each student 10 counters. Ask:
- *How many counters do you have? Line them up and count them.* (10)
- *Which counter is first in line? Which is last?*

What Can I Do?
Read the question and the response. Then read and discuss the examples. Ask:
- *How is the word* ten *like* tenth? *How is the word* four *like* fourth? (Both just add *-th* to the counting number to form the ordinal number.)
- Point out other similarities between the counting numbers and the ordinals; for example, *third* begins with the same two letters as *three*, and *fifth* begins with the same two letters as *five*.

Try It
Have students try to complete the matching without referring to the chart.

Power Practice
- Provide crayons. Have students complete the practice items. Then review each answer.

CHALLENGE

Lesson Goal
Read a story and draw on an analog clock the times mentioned in the story.

Introducing the Challenge
Draw three clock faces on the chalkboard, omitting the hands. Then read the sentences below aloud. Have students come to the chalkboard and draw hands to show the times in the sentences.

- *We started our trip at 9:15 in the morning.*
- *We stopped for lunch at 12:30 in the afternoon.*
- *At 2:45, we arrived at Grandma's house.*

Using the Challenge
- Read the directions aloud. Suggest that students circle the times they read in the story before drawing the hands on the clocks.
- Discuss the fact that 6:30 in the morning is shown the same on the clock as 6:30 in the evening.
- *If you looked at your clock, and it said 11:00, how would you know whether it was morning or night?* (by looking out a window, by considering what activities one is performing, and so on)

Fun Times

Read the story.
Draw hands on the clocks to show each time in order.

It's summer vacation! Jason and his sister, Katy, wake up at 6:30 in the morning. By 7:15 they are outside in the big field. They pick berries for breakfast and return to the house by 8:00. Dad makes berry pancakes.

By 11:15 or so, the pond is warm enough for swimming. Mom and Dad take the children for rides in the rowboat. Lunch is at 12:45 on the back deck. After that, everyone reads or naps. Around 2:30, it's time for a hike in the woods. Jason calls the dogs, and the family heads out for a nice walk.

Name_____

Calendar Clues

Mr. Lee's class has student helpers. Mr. Lee writes the helpers' names on the calendar.

Here is the calendar page for March. Columns run up and down. Rows run across.

Read the clues. Find out who is the helper.

MARCH

Sunday	Monday	Tuesday	Wednesday	Thursday	Friday	Saturday
			1	2 Tina	3	4
5	6 Lucia	7	8 Karif	9	10	11
12	13	14	15	16	17 Miles	18
19	20 Brittany	21	22 Franco	23 Miranda	24	25
26	27	28 Betsy	29	30	31 Claire	

1. Who is the helper in the second row of the fourth column? _____Karif_____

2. Who is the helper in the fourth row of the second column? _____Brittany_____

3. Who is the helper in the third row of the sixth column? _____Miles_____

4. Who is the helper in the fifth row of the third column? _____Betsy_____

5. Who is the helper in the first row of the fifth column? _____Tina_____

CHALLENGE

Lesson Goal
Identify dates on a calendar by giving their row and column locations.

Introducing the Challenge
Display the calendar page for the current month. Ask:

- *What is the first day of the month? What is the last day of the month?* (Answers will vary.)

- *How many rows are on the calendar page?* (Answers will vary.) *How many columns are on the calendar page?* (7)

Using the Challenge
- Read the directions aloud.

Suggest that students follow these steps:

- Find the column.

- Move your finger down the column to find the row.

- Write the person's name.

- Ask interested students to name the column and row for Lucia's birthday (second column, second row); Franco's birthday (fourth column, fourth row); Miranda's birthday (fifth column, fourth row); Claire's birthday (sixth column, fifth row); and Miki's birthday (seventh column, third row).

Add or Subtract

Write + or −. Then add or subtract.

1.

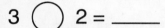

How many more starfish than clams?

3 ◯ 2 = _____

2.

How many in all?

2 ◯ 4 = _____

More and Fewer

Circle the group that has more.

3.

4.

Most and Fewest

Circle the group that has the least.

5.

6.

Subtract 2-Digit Numbers

Subtract.

7. $\begin{array}{r} 42 \\ -\ 10 \\ \hline \end{array}$ **8.** $\begin{array}{r} 66 \\ -\ 23 \\ \hline \end{array}$

9. $\begin{array}{r} 59 \\ -\ 37 \\ \hline \end{array}$ **10.** $\begin{array}{r} 30 \\ -\ \ 8 \\ \hline \end{array}$

Assessment Goal

This two-page assessment covers skills identified as necessary for success in Chapter 8 Data and Graphs. The first page assesses the major prerequisite skills for Cluster A. The second page assesses the major prerequisite skills for Cluster B. When the Cluster A and Cluster B prerequisite skills overlap, the skill(s) will be covered in only one section.

Getting Started

- Allow students time to look over the two pages of the assessment. Point out the labels that identify the skills covered.

- Have students find math vocabulary terms used in the assessment. List vocabulary terms on the board as students identify them. If necessary, review the meanings of all essential math vocabulary.

Introducing the Assessment

- Explain to students that these pages will help you know if they are ready to start a new chapter in their math textbooks.

- Students who have transferred from another school may not have been introduced to some of these skills. Encourage students to do their best and assure them you will help them learn any needed skills.

Cluster A Challenge

Those students who demonstrate mastery of the skills on this page will not need to use the reteaching worksheets. Instead, these students can do the Cluster A Challenge found on page 70.

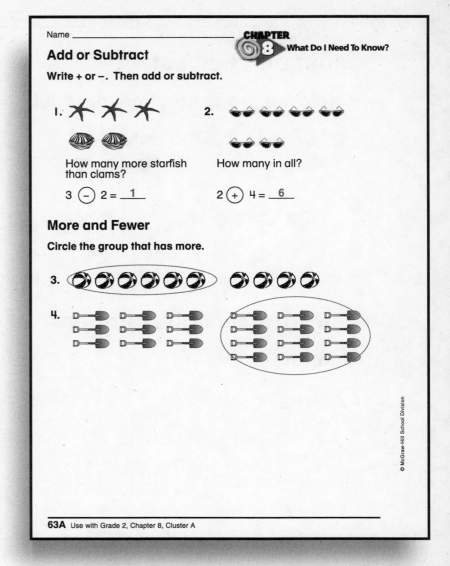

Name _____

Add or Subtract

Write + or −. Then add or subtract.

1. How many more starfish than clams?

$3 \ominus 2 = \underline{1}$

2. How many in all?

$2 \oplus 4 = \underline{6}$

More and Fewer

Circle the group that has more.

3.

4.

© McGraw-Hill School Division

63A Use with Grade 2, Chapter 8, Cluster A

CLUSTER A PREREQUISITE SKILLS

The skills listed in this chart are those identified as major prerequisite skills for students' success in the lessons in Cluster A of the chapter. Each skill is covered by one or more assessment items as shown in the middle column. The right column provides the page numbers for the lessons in this book that reteach the Cluster A prerequisite skills.

Skill Name	Assessment Items	Lesson Pages
Add or Subtract	1-2	64-65
More and Fewer	3-4	66

Name _____

Most and Fewest

Circle the group that has the least.

5.

6. (clam shells grouped in three sets, the middle group circled)

Subtract 2-Digit Numbers

Subtract.

7.　42
　− 10
　　32

8.　66
　− 23
　　43

9.　59
　− 37
　　22

10.　30
　−　8
　　22

Use with Grade 2, Chapter 8, Cluster B **63B**

CLUSTER B PREREQUISITE SKILLS

The skills listed in this chart are those identified as major prerequisite skills for students' success in the lessons in Cluster B of the chapter. Each skill is covered by one or more assessment items as shown in the middle column. The right column provides the page numbers for the lessons in this book that reteach the Cluster B prerequisite skills

Skill Name	Assessment Items	Lesson Pages
Most and Fewest	5-6	67
Subtract 2-Digit Numbers	7-10	68-69

Alternative Assessment Strategies

- Oral administration of the assessment is appropriate for younger students or those whose native language is not English. Read the skills title and directions one section at a time. Check students' understanding by asking them to tell you how they will do the first exercise in the group.

- For some skill types you may wish to use group administration. In this technique, a small group or pair of students complete the assessment together. Through their discussion, you will be able to decide if supplementary reteaching materials are needed.

Intervention Materials

If students are not successful with the prerequisite skills assessed on these pages, reteaching lessons have been created to help them make the transition into the chapter.

Item correlation charts showing the skills lessons suitable for reteaching the prerequisite skills are found beneath the reproductions of each page of the assessment.

Cluster B Challenge
Those students who demonstrate mastery of the skills on this page will not need to use the reteaching worksheets. Instead, these students can do the Cluster B Challenge found on page 71.

USING THE LESSON

Lesson Goal
- Choose the operation to solve a problem.

What the Student Needs to Know
- Recognize plus and minus signs.
- Use counters to model a problem.

Getting Started
Line up three girls and two boys. Ask:

- *How many students are there in all? How did you find out?* (5; put groups together; added)
- *How many more girls are there than boys? How did you find out?* (1 more; compared groups; subtracted)

What Can I Do?
Read the question and the response. Then read and discuss the examples. Ask:

- *What sign do you use in a number sentence to show how many in all?* (plus sign) *to show how many more?* (minus sign)
- *When you join two groups, do you add or subtract?* (add) *When you compare two groups, do you add or subtract?* (subtract)

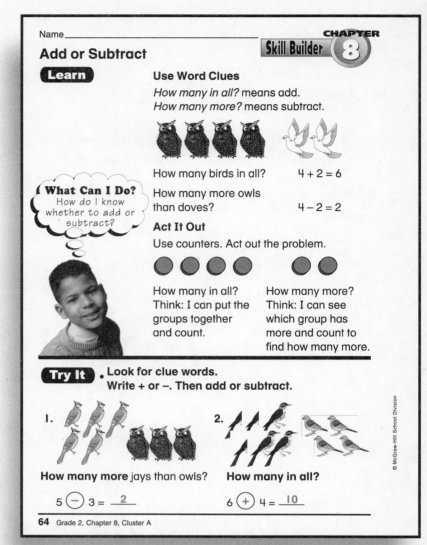

WHAT IF THE STUDENT CAN'T

Recognize Plus and Minus Signs
- Write number addition and subtraction sentences on the chalkboard. Ask students to circle the sign in each addition sentence. Repeat the activity, asking the student to circle the sign in each subtraction sentence. Then have the student solve the problem.

Use Counters to Model a Problem
- Give the student 20 counters. Ask the student to model number sentences like these: $2 + 3 = 5$, $16 - 9 = 7$, $4 + 8 = 12$, $9 - 5 = 4$, $6 + 8 = 14$, $11 - 2 = 9$.
- Ask the student to use counters to model problems 3–10.

Name_____

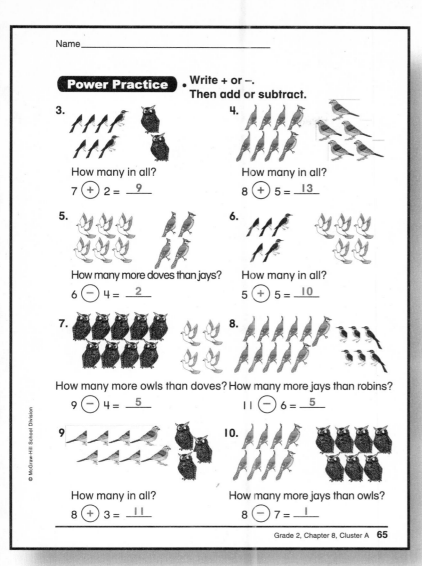

3.

How many in all?

$7 \oplus 2 = \underline{9}$

4.

How many in all?

$8 \oplus 5 = \underline{13}$

5.

How many more doves than jays?

$6 \ominus 4 = \underline{2}$

6.

How many in all?

$5 \oplus 5 = \underline{10}$

7.

How many more owls than doves?

$9 \ominus 4 = \underline{5}$

8.

How many more jays than robins?

$11 \ominus 6 = \underline{5}$

9.

How many in all?

$8 \oplus 3 = \underline{11}$

10.

How many more jays than owls?

$8 \ominus 7 = \underline{1}$

© McGraw-Hill School Division

Grade 2, Chapter 8, Cluster A **65**

USING THE LESSON

Try It
Remind students that each item requires two steps: (1) choosing a plus or minus sign and (2) solving the number sentence.

Power Practice
- You may want to suggest that students go through the exercises first, looking for clue words and writing the plus or minus signs. When they have completed that task, they may go back and add or subtract to solve the number sentences.
- Have students complete the practice items. Then review each answer.

Learn with Partners & Parents
Students can practice choosing the operation by using spoons and forks.
- Display several spoons and forks. Ask:
- *How many spoons and forks are there in all? Do you add or subtract to find out?* (add)
- *Are there more spoons or more forks? How many more? Do you add or subtract to find out?* (subtract)

WHAT IF THE STUDENT CAN'T

Complete the Power Practice
- Have the student read aloud any problems they answered incorrectly and repeat the clue words. Then have the student solve the problem again.

- Watch for students who choose the operation correctly but need additional help with addition and subtraction facts.

Lesson Goal
- Compare two groups.

What the Student Needs to Know
- Recognize the meaning of "more" and "fewer."
- Match one-to-one.
- Count to 12.

Getting Started
Line up four girls and five boys. Ask them to pair off. Then ask:

- *Can all the girls and boys pair off? Who is left over? Are there more girls or more boys?* (more boys)

Repeat using six girls and five boys. Then Ask:

- *How could we use one-to-one matching to see whether there are more boys or girls in our class?* (Line up boys and girls and have them pair off. The group with students left over has more.)

What Can I Do?
Read the question and the response. Then read and discuss the examples. Ask:

- *How can we tell if there are more ants or more spiders?* (Draw a line to match one ant with one spider and see if there are any ants or spiders left over.)

Then Ask:

- *What is another way to compare groups?* (Count how many are in each group. Write a number next to each ladybug and each grasshopper and compare numbers.)

Try It
Have students look back at the ants and spiders above to see how to draw lines to match one-to-one.

Power Practice
- Tell students they may use either strategy to complete items 2–3.
- Have students complete the practice items. Then review each answer.

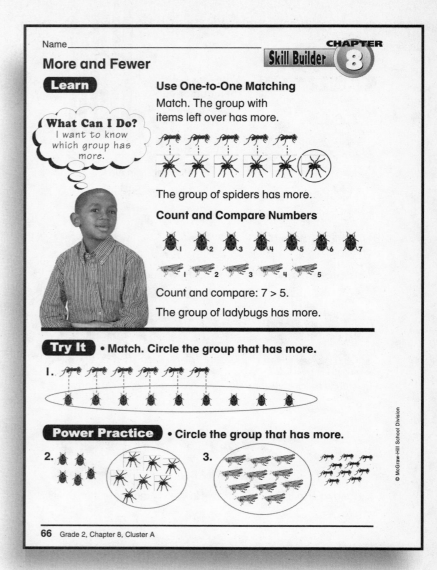

Name_____

More and Fewer

Learn

What Can I Do? I want to know which group has more.

Use One-to-One Matching
Match. The group with items left over has more.

The group of spiders has more.

Count and Compare Numbers

Count and compare: 7 > 5.

The group of ladybugs has more.

Try It • Match. Circle the group that has more.

1.

Power Practice • Circle the group that has more.

2.   3.

© McGraw-Hill School Division

66   Grade 2, Chapter 8, Cluster A

WHAT IF THE STUDENT CAN'T

Recognize the Meaning of "More" and "Fewer"
Ask the student the following questions that involve the concepts *more* or *fewer*. Have the student find the solution to each.

- *Count the crayons and pencils in your desk. Are there more or fewer crayons than pencils?*
- *Think about the number of school days in a week compared to the number of weekend days. Are there more or fewer school days than weekend days?*

Match One-to-One
- Distribute attribute block squares in two colors. Have the student make pairs to determine which group has more.

Count to 12
- Give the student an egg carton and 12 counters. Have the student drop one counter into each compartment of the egg carton, counting as he or she does so.

Complete the Power Practice
- If the student has not used one-to-one matching, ask the student to draw lines to pair up items in the two groups. Remind the student that the group with items left over has more.

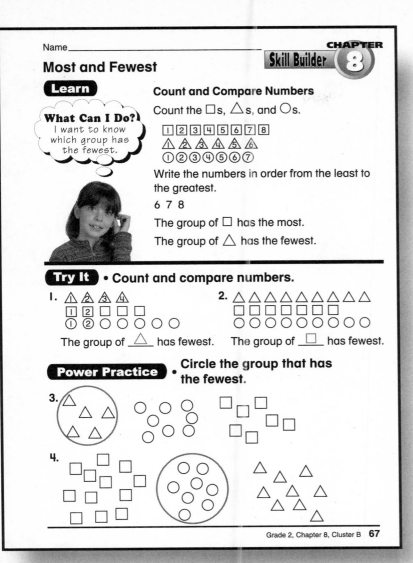

Most and Fewest

Learn

What Can I Do?
I want to know which group has the fewest.

Count and Compare Numbers

Count the □s, △s, and ○s.

① ② ③ ④ ⑤ ⑥ ⑦ ⑧
△ △ △ △ △ △
① ② ③ ④ ⑤ ⑥ ⑦

Write the numbers in order from the least to the greatest.

6 7 8

The group of □ has the most.

The group of △ has the fewest.

Try It • Count and compare numbers.

1. △ △ △ △
   ① ② □ □ □
   ① ② ○ ○ ○ ○

   The group of △ has fewest.

2. △ △ △ △ △ △ △ △ △
   □ □ □ □ □ □ □
   ○ ○ ○ ○ ○ ○ ○ ○ ○ ○

   The group of □ has fewest.

Power Practice • Circle the group that has the fewest.

3.

4.

WHAT IF THE STUDENT CAN'T

Recognize the Meaning of "Most" and "Fewest"

Ask students the following questions that involve the concepts *most* or *fewest*. Have students find the solution to each.

• Give the student red, blue, and yellow counters. Ask: *Which group has the most counters? Which group has the fewest counters?*

• Give the student groups of play pennies, nickels, and dimes. Ask: *Which group has the most coins? Which group has the fewest coins?*

Match One-to-One

• Distribute attribute blocks in three shapes. Have the student use one-to-one matchup to determine which group has the most shapes and which group has the fewest.

Complete the Power Practice

• If the student has not used one-to-one matching, ask the student to draw circles containing one item from each of the three groups. Remind the student that the group with no items left over has the fewest.

• Have students count the items in each group aloud before identifying the group with the fewest.

Lesson Goal

• Compare more than two groups.

What the Student Needs to Know

• Recognize the meaning of "most" and "fewest."

• Match one-to-one.

Getting Started

On a felt board, display three circles, four triangles, and five squares. Ask:

• *Which group has more, the circles or the triangles?* (triangles)

• *Which group has more, the triangles or the squares?* (squares)

• *Which group has the most?* (squares)

What Can I Do?

Read the question and the response. Then read and discuss the examples.

• Explain that the words *more* and *fewer* are used to compare two groups. When you compare three groups or more, you use the words *most* and *fewest*.

• Ask studenst to tell why the words *most* and *fewest* are used in the example. (Three groups of objects are being compared.)

Try It

Point out to students that the question asks them to find the group with the fewest items.

Power Practice

• Suggest to students that they should write down the number of objects in each group.

• Have students complete the practice items. Then review each answer.

Lesson Goal

- Subtract 2-digit numbers, with and without regrouping.

What the Student Needs to Know

- Recognize when regrouping is necessary.
- Rename tens and ones as ones.
- Add 2-digit numbers, with and without regrouping.

Getting Started

Give each group of students 5 tens models and 15 ones models. Ask them to show these number sentences:

- 55 – 25 = ? (30)
- 55 – 26 = ? (29)

Discuss the regrouping students had to do to complete the second example: regrouping 1 ten and 5 ones as 15 ones and then subtracting 6 ones from 15 ones.

What Can I Do?

Read the question and the response. Then read and discuss the examples. Ask:

- *How can you tell by looking at two numbers whether you'll have to regroup?* (If the number of ones in the lesser number is greater than the number of ones in the greater number, you will have to regroup.)

- *Why does it work to check subtraction by adding?* (In subtraction, you take a lesser number away from a greater number. In addition, you add the two lesser numbers to form the greater number.)

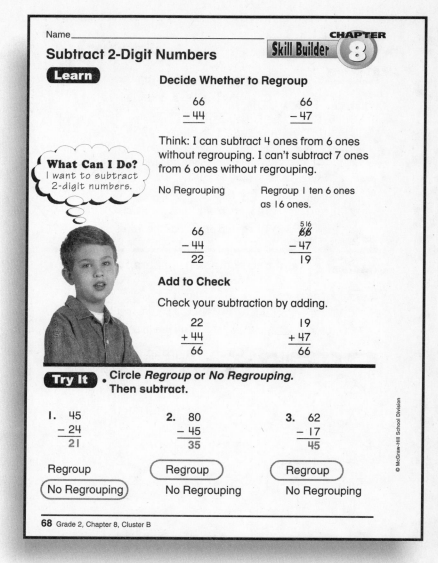

WHAT IF THE STUDENT CAN'T

Recognize When Regrouping Is Necessary

- Review items 4–18 and have the student tell by looking at the ones digits which items require regrouping.

Rename Tens and Ones as Ones

Distribute tens and ones models. Have the student show these regroupings:

- *Regroup 1 ten 6 ones.* (16 ones)
- *Regroup 4 tens 5 ones.* (3 tens 15 ones)
- *Regroup 3 tens 2 ones.* (2 tens 12 ones)
- *Regroup 2 tens 4 ones.* (1 ten 14 ones)

Add 2-Digit Numbers, With and Without Regrouping

- Provide the student with number cards 0–99. Have the student draw two cards, write the numbers, and add them. Repeat several times.

Name_____

Power Practice • Subtract.
Check by adding.

4. 22 −8 14	**5.** 83 −12 71	**6.** 76 −27 49
7. 43 −25 18	**8.** 94 −33 61	**9.** 67 −7 60
10. 32 −18 14	**11.** 65 −25 40	**12.** 46 −17 29
13. 94 −65 29	**14.** 54 −20 34	**15.** 58 −39 19
16. 23 −15 8	**17.** 67 −28 39	**18.** 55 −51 4

© McGraw-Hill School Division

Grade 2, Chapter 8, Cluster B **69**

Try It
- Remind students to look at the ones digit of each number to decide whether to regroup or not.
- Make sure that students complete both steps: (1) Circle "Regroup" or "No Regrouping" and (2) Complete the subtraction.

Power Practice
- Remind students to check their subtraction by adding.
- Have students complete the practice items. Then discuss their answers.

WHAT IF THE STUDENT CAN'T

Complete the Power Practice
- Review with the student any exercises that were done incorrectly one-on-one. Have the student explain how he or she knew whether or not to regroup. Then watch as the student completes the subtraction again. Look for problems that involve regrouping, alignment of digits, or adding instead of subtracting.

Lesson Goal

- Use logical reasoning to complete the bars on a bar graph.

Introducing the Challenge

Give students this exercise in logic before assigning the worksheet.

- *Alex is 5 years older than Kim.*
- *Kim is 4 years older than Caleb.*
- *Caleb is 3 years old. How old are Kim and Alex? (7 and 12)*

Talk about the logical steps to use when solving such a problem:

1. Start with the known number. (Caleb is 3.)
2. Proceed based on that known number. (Kim is 4 years older than 3.)
3. Continue until all parts of the problem are solved.

Using the Challenge

- Read the directions aloud. Suggest that students follow these steps to complete the activity.
- Write the choices—Seashore, Mountains, Lake, City.
- Start with the known number. Then figure out the number of people who chose each one. Write it next to the name of the choice.
- Use your list to complete the bar graph.
- Check your bar graph against the clues.

Name_____

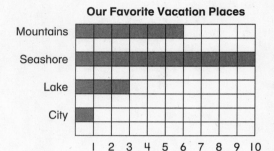

Mystery Bar Graph

Use the clues to fill in the bars on the bar graph.

Our Favorite Vacation Places

Mountains
Seashore
Lake
City

1 2 3 4 5 6 7 8 9 10

Clues:

20 people were in the tally.

Each person chose one place.

4 more people chose Seashore than Mountains.

3 more people chose Mountains than Lake.

2 more people chose Lake than City.

1 person chose City.

© McGraw-Hill School Division

Name_____

3-Way Data

Use this information.
Complete the tally, the bar graph, and the pictograph.

1. 4 people have dogs.
2. 6 people have cats.
3. 2 people have fish.
4. 1 person has a turtle.
5. 1 person has a snake.

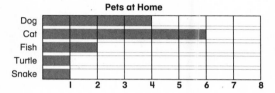

Pets at Home	
Dog	||||
Cat	⁄⁄⁄⁄ |
Fish	||
Turtle	|
Snake	|

Pets at Home

	1	2	3	4	5	6	7	8
Dog								
Cat								
Fish								
Turtle								
Snake								

Pets at Home	
Dog	☺ ☺ ☺ ☺
Cat	☺ ☺ ☺ ☺ ☺ ☺
Fish	☺ ☺
Turtle	☺
Snake	☺

Key: ☺ = 1 person

CHALLENGE

Lesson Goal

- Complete a tally, pictograph, and bar graph for given data.

Introducing the Challenge

Distribute the activity. Ask:

- *What information is given?* (Numbers of people who own different pets.)
- *What are the different ways you are to show that information?* (in a tally, in a pictograph, and in a bar graph)
- *What symbol are you to use on the pictograph to stand for 1 person?* (smiley face)
- *What is the greatest number shown on the bar graph?* (8)

Using the Challenge

When all students have completed the tally and graphs, ask these questions:

- *Which pet was the most popular?* (cats)
- *How many more people had dogs than had fish?* (2 more)
- *Did you use the tally, the pictograph, or the bar graph to answer these questions?* (Answers will vary.)

Explore Length

How long is each one?

1.

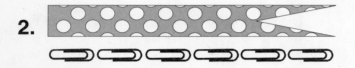 _____

2.  _____

Explore Capacity

Circle the one that holds more.

3.

Explore Weight

Circle the one that is heavier.

4.

5.

Adding Three or More Numbers

Add.

6. 5 + 1 + 3 + 2 = _____

Name_____

Compare Numbers

Use the number line. Circle the number that is greater.

7. 12   22

8. 30   13

9. 16   18

10. 28   24

CHAPTER 9 PRE-CHAPTER ASSESSMENT

Assessment Goal

This two-page assessment covers skills identified as necessary for success in Chapter 9 Measurement. The first page assesses the major prerequisite skills for Cluster A. The second page assesses the major prerequisite skills for Cluster B. When the Cluster A and Cluster B prerequisite skills overlap, the skill(s) will be covered in only one section.

Getting Started

- Allow students time to look over the two pages of the assessment. Point out the labels that identify the skills covered.

- Have students find math vocabulary terms used in the assessment. List vocabulary terms on the board as students identify them. If necessary, review the meanings of all essential math vocabulary.

Introducing the Assessment

- Explain to students that these pages will help you know if they are ready to start a new chapter in their math textbooks.

- Students who have transferred from another school may not have been introduced to some of these skills. Encourage students to do their best and assure them you will help them learn any needed skills.

Cluster A Challenge

Those students who demonstrate mastery of the skills on this page will not need to use the reteaching worksheets. Instead, these students can do the Cluster A Challenge found on page 82.

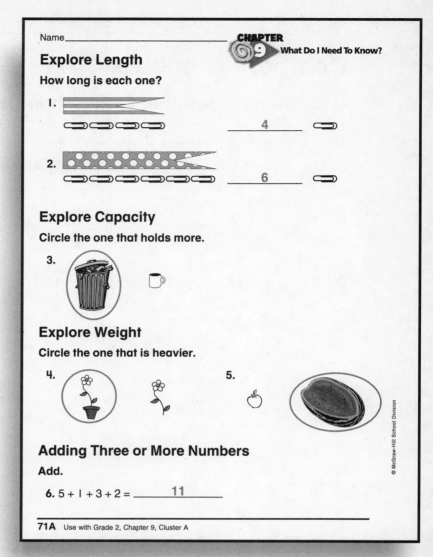

Name_____

Explore Length

How long is each one?

1. _____ 4 _____

2. _____ 6 _____

Explore Capacity

Circle the one that holds more.

3.

Explore Weight

Circle the one that is heavier.

4.   5.

Adding Three or More Numbers

Add.

6. $5 + 1 + 3 + 2 = $ _____11_____

71A Use with Grade 2, Chapter 9, Cluster A

CLUSTER A PREREQUISITE SKILLS

The skills listed in this chart are those identified as major prerequisite skills for students' success in the lessons in Cluster A of the chapter. Each skill is covered by one or more assessment items as shown in the middle column. The right column provides the page numbers for the lessons in this book that reteach the Cluster A prerequisite skills.

Skill Name	Assessment Items	Lesson Pages
Explore Length	1-2	72-73
Explore Capacity	3	74-75
Explore Weight	4-5	76-77
Adding Three or More Numbers	6	78-79

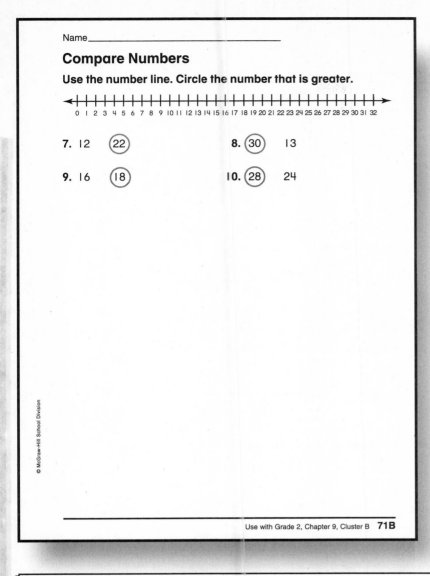

Name_____

Compare Numbers

Use the number line. Circle the number that is greater.

0 1 2 3 4 5 6 7 8 9 10 11 12 13 14 15 16 17 18 19 20 21 22 23 24 25 26 27 28 29 30 31 32

7. 12   (22)   **8.** (30)   13

9. 16   (18)   **10.** (28)   24

CLUSTER B PREREQUISITE SKILLS

The skills listed in this chart are those identified as major prerequisite skills for students' success in the lessons in Cluster B of the chapter. Each skill is covered by one or more assessment items as shown in the middle column. The right column provides the page numbers for the lessons in this book that reteach the Cluster B prerequisite skills

Skill Name	Assessment Items	Lesson Pages
Compare Numbers	7-10	80-81

Alternative Assessment Strategies

- Oral administration of the assessment is appropriate for younger students or those whose native language is not English. Read the skills title and directions one section at a time. Check students' understanding by asking them to tell you how they will do the first exercise in the group.

- For some skill types you may wish to use group administration. In this technique, a small group or pair of students complete the assessment together. Through their discussion, you will be able to decide if supplementary reteaching materials are needed.

Intervention Materials

If students are not successful with the prerequisite skills assessed on these pages, reteaching lessons have been created to help them make the transition into the chapter.

Item correlation charts showing the skills lessons suitable for reteaching the prerequisite skills are found beneath the reproductions of each page of the assessment.

Cluster B Challenge

Those students who demonstrate mastery of the skills on this page will not need to use the reteaching worksheets. Instead, these students can do the Cluster B Challenge found on page 83.

Lesson Goal
- Measure length using nonstandard units.

What the Student Needs to Know
- Use a measuring tool.
- Count to ten.

Getting Started
Draw a horizontal line on the chalkboard. Ask:

- *How could I measure this line using only chalkboard erasers?* (Line up erasers from the left to the right ends of the line; then count the erasers.)

Demonstrate this technique.

What Can I Do?
Read the question and the response. Then read and discuss the examples. Ask:

- *What does it mean to "line things up" at the left edge?* (Make sure the left edges of the measurement tool and the object being measured are even.)

- *Why is it important to line things up when you measure?* (It helps you get an accurate measurement.)

Try It
Point out that a pencil that is 3 clips long will not be 3 cubes long. A pencil that is 6 cubes long will not be 6 clips long. Clips and cubes are different sizes; using them results in different measurements.

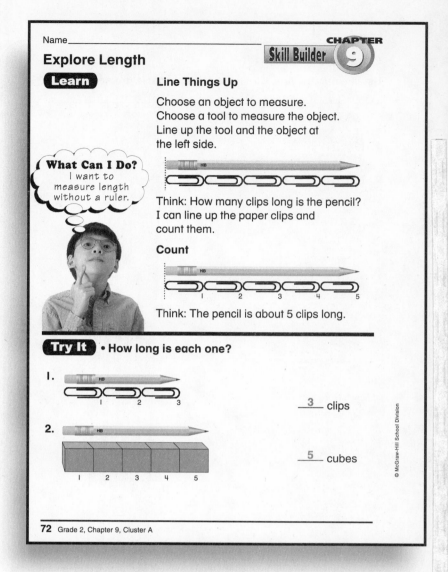

Name_____

Explore Length

Learn

Line Things Up

Choose an object to measure.
Choose a tool to measure the object.
Line up the tool and the object at the left side.

What Can I Do? I want to measure length without a ruler.

Think: How many clips long is the pencil? I can line up the paper clips and count them.

Count

Think: The pencil is about 5 clips long.

Try It • How long is each one?

1.

_3_ clips

2.

_5_ cubes

© McGraw-Hill School Division

WHAT IF THE STUDENT CAN'T

Use a Measuring Tool
- Present the student with a handful of paper clips and a book. Have the student use the clips to measure the length of the book. Make alignment corrections, if necessary. Repeat with a book of a different size.

Count to Ten
- Give the student 20 counters. Ask the student to count and separate out 10 counters.
- Line up 8 paper clips and have the student count them. Repeat with 6, 9, and 5 paper clips.

Name_____

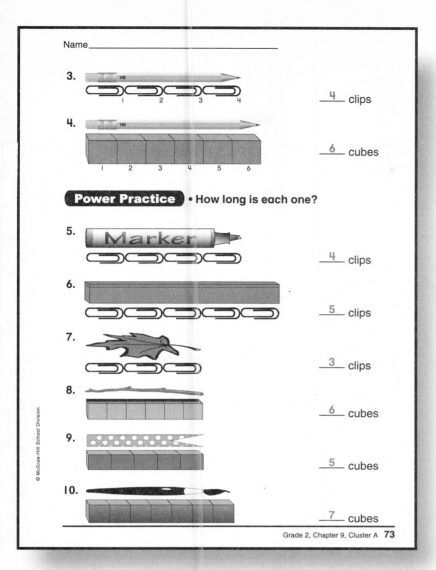

3. _____4_____ clips

4. _____6_____ cubes

Power Practice • How long is each one?

5. Marker _____4_____ clips

6. _____5_____ clips

7. _____3_____ clips

8. _____6_____ cubes

9. _____5_____ cubes

10. _____7_____ cubes

Power Practice

- Point out that the measuring tools are aligned on the left side of the object being measured.
- Have students complete the practice items. Then review each answer.

Learn with Partners & Parents

Give students a handful of index cards and have them follow these Scavenger Hunt directions.

- *Find a chair. Measure the length of the seat using index cards. Write the measurement to the nearest wholecard.*
- *Find a table. Measure its length using index cards. Write the measurement to the nearest whole card.*
- *Find a window. Measure its width using index cards. Write the measurement to the nearest whole card.*
- *Tell which object was longest and which was shortest.*

WHAT IF THE STUDENT CAN'T

Complete the Power Practice

- Have the student demonstrate how he or she solved any incorrect problems. See whether the student counted incorrectly or did not understand how to use nonstandard units of measure.

Lesson Goal

- Identify the object that holds more or less.

What the Student Needs to Know

- Recognize the meaning of "more" and "less."
- Recognize the meaning of "longer," "wider," and "deeper."

Getting Started

Hold up a teacup and a mug or two glasses of different sizes. Ask:

- *If you were very thirsty, which one would you rather have? Why?* (the bigger one, because it holds more)
- *How can you tell that the bigger one holds more?* (It is taller or deeper; it is wider than the other one.)

Name_____

Explore Capacity

Learn

Use Your Imagination

Look at the pictures.
Imagine using each one.

What Can I Do?
I want to know which one holds more.

Think: When I take a bath, I use a lot of water. When I fill a glass, I use a little water. The bathtub holds more water than the glass.

Compare Other Measurements

Think: The tub is longer than the glass. It is wider than the glass, too. It is also deeper than the glass. So, the tub must hold more than the glass.

Try It • Circle the one that holds more.

1.

2.

© McGraw-Hill School Division

74 Grade 2, Chapter 9, Cluster A

WHAT IF THE STUDENT CAN'T

Recognize the Meaning of "More" and "Less"

Ask the student questions that involve the concepts *more* and *less*.

- *Do you drink more milk than juice each day?*
- *Do you use less water to bathe than you do to brush your teeth?*

Recognize the Meaning of "Longer," "Wider," and "Deeper"

Ask the student questions like these:

- *Which is longer, your finger or your arm?*
- *Which is wider, your smile or your thumb?*
- *Which is deeper, a puddle or a pond?*

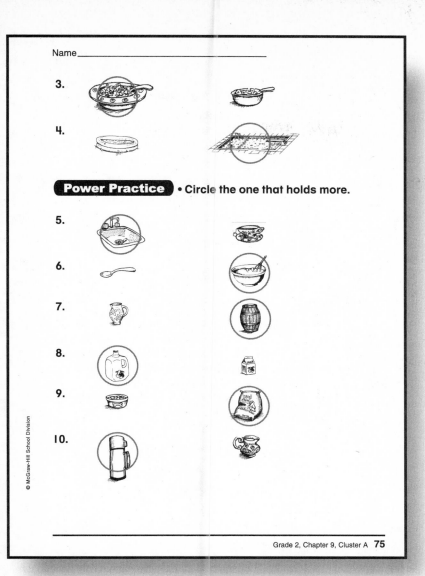

Name_____

3.

4.

Power Practice • Circle the one that holds more.

5.

6.

7.

8.

9.

10.

© McGraw-Hill School Division

What Can I Do?
Read the question and the response. Then read and discuss the examples. Say:

- *Use your imagination. Which would hold more, a fishtank or a lake?* (a lake)
- *Which would be longer, a fishtank or a lake?* (a lake)
- *Which would be wider, a fishtank or a lake?* (a lake)
- *Which would be deeper, a fishtank or a lake?* (a lake)

Try It
Ask students to identify the objects in each picture before they begin the exercise.

Power Practice
- Have students complete the practice items. Then review each answer.

WHAT IF THE STUDENT CAN'T

Complete the Power Practice
- Make sure the student is able to identify the objects in each picture.
- Discuss how each object may be used. Then ask the student to tell which one holds more.

Lesson Goal

- Identify the object that is heavier or lighter.

What the Student Needs to Know

- Recognize the meaning of "heavy" and "light."
- Use a balance.

Getting Started

Place two equal weights on either side of a balance. Say:

- *When the balance is balanced, the weights are the same.*

Replace one weight with a heavier weight. Say:

- *When one weight is heavier, the balance tips down.*
- *What will happen if I take one weight off?* (The balance will tip toward the other weight.)

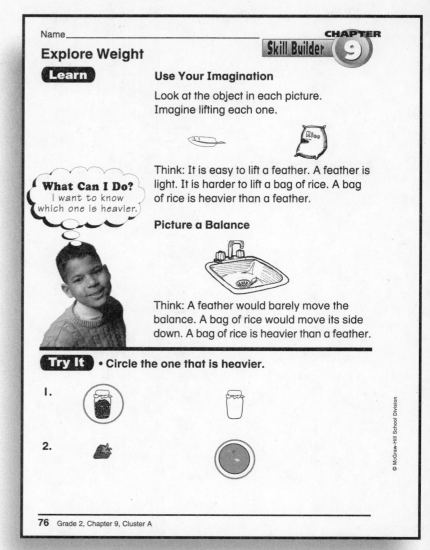

Name_____

Explore Weight

Skill Builder — CHAPTER 9

Learn

Use Your Imagination

Look at the object in each picture.
Imagine lifting each one.

What Can I Do? I want to know which one is heavier.

Think: It is easy to lift a feather. A feather is light. It is harder to lift a bag of rice. A bag of rice is heavier than a feather.

Picture a Balance

Think: A feather would barely move the balance. A bag of rice would move its side down. A bag of rice is heavier than a feather.

Try It • Circle the one that is heavier.

1.

2.

© McGraw-Hill School Division

76 Grade 2, Chapter 9, Cluster A

WHAT IF THE STUDENT CAN'T

Recognize the Meanings of "Heavy" and "Light"

Ask the student questions like these:

- *Would you call an elephant heavy or light?* (heavy)
- *Would you call a bird heavy or light?* (light)
- *Which is heavier, a baby or an adult?* (an adult)
- *Which is lighter, a bike or a car?* (a bike)

Use a Balance

- Provide a balance and several small objects. Have the student practice guessing which objects will move the balance most and placing them on the balance to test each guess.

Name_____

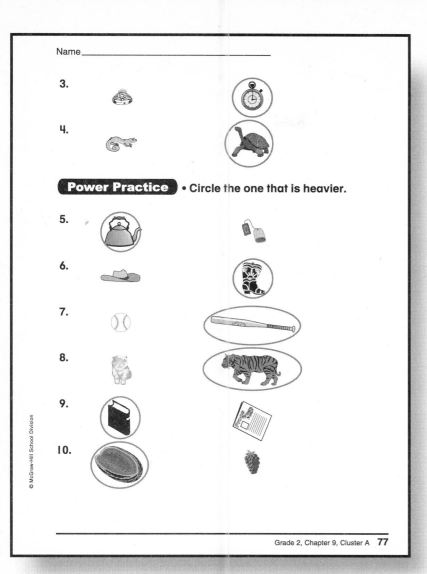

3.

4.

Power Practice • Circle the one that is heavier.

5.

6.

7.

8.

9.

10.

What Can I Do?
Read the question and the response. Then read and discuss the examples. Say:

• *Use your imagination. Which would be heavier, an empty bucket or a bucket full of sand?* (a bucket full of sand)

• *Which would be heavier, a dry swimsuit or a wet swimsuit?* (a wet swimsuit)

Try It
Make sure students can identify the objects in each picture before they begin the exercise.

Power Practice
• Have students complete the practice items. Then review each answer.

WHAT IF THE STUDENT CAN'T

Complete the Power Practice
• Make sure the student is able to identify the objects for each pair.
• Have the student close his or her eyes and imagine lifting each item in a pair; for example, a teapot and a teabag. Which is heavier? How does the student know?

Lesson Goal
• Add three or more numbers.

What the Student Needs to Know
• Make 10.
• Use the Commutative Property of Addition.

Getting Started
On the chalkboard, draw the following:

O O

O O O

O O O O

O O O O O

Ask:

• *How could you add all four groups of circles?* (Add the first two groups; then add the third group to that sum; then add the fourth group to that sum.)

Have the students find the sum. (14)

What Can I Do?
Read the question and the response. Then read and discuss the examples. Ask:

• *Why does it help to find 10?* (It's easy to add 10 to other numbers.)

• *Why can you check addition by adding the numbers in a different direction?* (Changing the order of addends does not change the sum.)

Name_____

Adding Three or More Numbers   Skill Builder

Learn

Look for 10

Look for numbers that add up to 10.   1
Add those numbers first.   3
Then add the other numbers   4
   +7

What Can I Do? I want to add 3 or more numbers.

Think: $3 + 7 = 10$, $1 + 4 = 5$, $10 + 5 = 15$.

Add in Stages

Add the first two numbers.   4
Then add the third number.   2
Then add the fourth number.   1
Check by adding the numbers   +6
in a different direction.

Think: $4 + 2 = 6$, $6 + 1 = 7$, $7 + 6 = 13$.
$6 + 1 + 2 + 4 = 13$

Try It • Look for 10.
   Add.

1.   5
   4
   6]
   +2
   17

2.   5
   2
   1
   +8]
   16

3. $1 + 9 + 7 =$ __17__

4. $5 + 4 + 5 + 4 =$ __18__

WHAT IF THE STUDENT CAN'T

Make 10
• Give the student ten counters. Have him or her group the counters in as many ways as possible to make two groups that add up to 10. (1 + 9, 2 + 8, . . . 9 + 1)

Use the Commutative Property of Addition
Ask the student questions like these:

• *If 3 + 4 = 7, what is 4 + 3?* (7)

• *If 9 + 2 = 11, what is 2 + 9?* (11)

Have the student model similar addition pairs using counters.

Name_____

Power Practice • Add.

5.	6	6.	2	7.	5
	4		2		7
	3		9		+5
	+7		+8		17
	20		21		

8.	4	9.	3	10.	4
	5		7		4
	1		+7		4
	+6		17		+8
	16				20

11. $3 + 6 + 1 = \underline{10}$

12. $4 + 7 + 3 = \underline{14}$

13. $9 + 1 + 4 + 3 = \underline{17}$

14. $5 + 5 + 6 + 2 = \underline{18}$

15. $2 + 3 + 4 + 5 + 6 + 7 = \underline{27}$

© McGraw-Hill School Division

Try It

• Remind students that they will not always be able to find 10 in an addition problem. Items 1–4, however, all include 10.

• Suggest that students check their answers by adding in the other direction.

Power Practice

• Remind students to chesk their addition by adding in the other direction.

• Have students complete the practice items. Then discuss their answers.

WHAT IF THE STUDENT CAN'T

Complete the Power Practice

• Have students work out incorrect problems as you observe. Watch for students who add only three out of four addends or who cannot hold a sum in their heads long enough to add it to the next number.

• Provide counters for students to use to model any incorrect problems.

Lesson Goal
• Compare numbers to 99.

What the Student Needs to Know
• Recognize the meaning of "greater" and "less."
• Read a number line.
• Read a place-value chart.

Getting Started
Have students count aloud from 20 to 30. Ask:
• *Which numbers that you said are greater than 25? (26, 27, . . . 30)*

What Can I Do?
Read the question and the response. Then read and discuss the examples. Ask:
• *If 15 is to the right of 13, which number is greater? (15)*
• *If 13 is to the left of 15, which number is less? (13)*
• *How can you use place value to compare the numbers 13 and 15?* (Look at the tens digits. Since they are the same, look at the ones digits. 5 ones is greater than 3 ones, so 15 is greater than 13.)

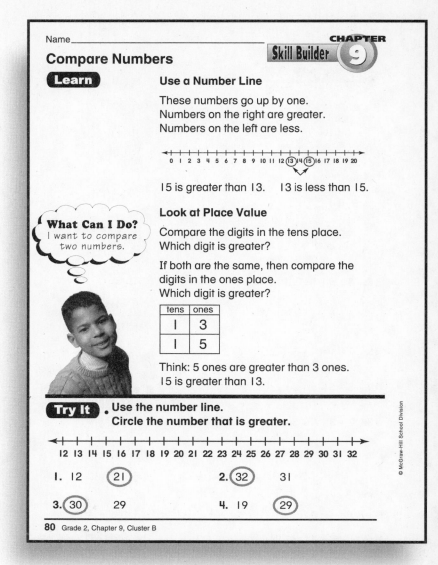

Name_____

Compare Numbers

Learn

Use a Number Line

These numbers go up by one.
Numbers on the right are greater.
Numbers on the left are less.

0 1 2 3 4 5 6 7 8 9 10 11 12 (13) (15) 16 17 18 19 20

15 is greater than 13.   13 is less than 15.

What Can I Do?
I want to compare two numbers.

Look at Place Value

Compare the digits in the tens place. Which digit is greater?

If both are the same, then compare the digits in the ones place. Which digit is greater?

tens	ones
1	3
1	5

Think: 5 ones are greater than 3 ones.
15 is greater than 13.

Try It . Use the number line.
Circle the number that is greater.

12 13 14 15 16 17 18 19 20 21 22 23 24 25 26 27 28 29 30 31 32

1. 12 (21)   2. (32) 31

3. (30) 29   4. 19 (29)

© McGraw-Hill School Division

80 Grade 2, Chapter 9, Cluster B

WHAT IF THE STUDENT CAN'T

Recognize the Meaning of "Greater" and "Less"
• Give the student a pile of counters. Ask the student to separate the pile into two piles, count the counters, and tell which number is greater and which is less.

Read a Number Line
Draw a 0–10 number line on the chalkboard, omitting several numbers. Say:
• *Fill in the missing numbers in order.*
• *Which number is least? (0)*
• *Which numbers is greatest? (10)*
• *Which numbers are less than 4? (0, 1, 2, 3,)*
• *Which numbers are greater than 7? (8, 9, 10)*

Name_____

Power Practice • Circle the number that is greater.

5. 45   (54)   6. (33)   23

7. 56   (66)   8. 69   (70)

9. (97)   88   10. (17)   16

11. 19   (29)   12. (80)   79

13. (48)   47   14. 47   (57)

15. 73   (83)   16. (82)   28

17. 44   (55)   18. (50)   5

19. 26   (28)   20. (59)   58

Grade 2, Chapter 9, Cluster B   **81**

Try It
Remind students to use the number line to determine which number is greater.

Power Practice
- Have students complete the practice items. Then review each answer. Discuss the strategies students used to find the greater number.
- Extend the practice by having students name a number that is greater than either of the numbers shown in each pair. For example, for exercise 5, 55 is greater than 45 or 54.

WHAT IF THE STUDENT CAN'T

Read a Place-Value Chart
- Write these numbers in a place-value chart: 42, 24, 31, 13, 48, 84. Have the student identify the number of tens and ones in each number and write the two-digit number.

Complete the Power Practice
- Discuss each incorrect answer. Have the student identify the number of tens and ones in each number, compare tens, and then compare ones.

CHALLENGE

Lesson Goal

- Use logical reasoning to solve a problem involving length.

Introducing the Challenge

Give students this exercise in logic before assigning the activity.

- *Andrea has 5 cents more than Cody.*
- *Bill has 3 cents less than Andrea.*
- *Cody has 8 cents. How much do Andrea and Bill have?* (Andrea has 13 cents; Bill has 10 cents.)

Talk about the logical steps to use when solving such a problem:

1. Start with the known number. (Cody has 8 cents.)

2. Proceed based on that known number. (Andrea has 5 cents more than Cody's 8 cents, which equals 13 cents.)

3. Continue until all the parts of the problem are solved.

Using the Challenge

- Read the directions aloud. Suggest that students follow these steps to complete the activity.
- Write the people's names— Abner, Beth, Celia, and Danny.
- Start with the known amount.
- Use that number to find the next, related number.
- Continue until the problem is solved.
- Check by reading the clues again and testing them against your answers.

Logical Length

Abner, Beth, Celia, and Danny have a frog-jumping contest. Use the clues and a ruler. Draw lines that show how far each frog jumped. Then answer the questions.

Clues

1. Abner's frog jumped 3 inches.

2. Beth's frog jumped 2 inches farther than Celia's frog.

3. Celia's frog jumped the same distance as Abner's frog.

4. Danny's frog jumped 1 inch farther than Abner's frog.

Abner's

Beth's

Celia's

Danny's

Questions

1. How far did each child's frog jump?

   Abner's: __3__ inches   Beth's: __5__ inches

   Celia's: __3__ inches   Danny's: __4__ inches

2. Which frog won? _____ Beth _____ 's frog

Five O'Clock Temperature

Read the weather reports.
Draw the line in the thermometer.
Show the temperature at 5:00.

February 24. The temperature at dawn was 5 degrees F. It went up 10 degrees by noon. By 5:00, it had dropped 5 degrees.

February 25. The temperature at dawn was 12 degrees F. It went up 8 degrees by noon and dropped 5 degrees by 5:00.

February 26. The temperature at dawn was 15 degrees F. It went up 15 degrees by noon and dropped 5 degrees by 5:00.

February 27. The temperature at dawn was 20 degrees F. It went up 12 degrees by noon and dropped 7 degrees by 5:00.

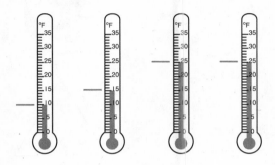

February 24   February 25   February 26   February 27

© McGraw-Hill School Division

CHALLENGE

Lesson Goal
- Find a temperature by adding and subtracting degrees.

Introducing the Challenge
On the chalkboard, draw a 0–10 number line. Say:

- *Start at 0. Go up 4. Go down 3. Where are you?* (1)
- *Start at 5. Go up 4. Go down 3. Where are you?* (6)
- *Start at 3. Go up 5. Go down 1. Where are you?* (7)

Using the Challenge
- Tell students that they may use addition and subtraction to solve the problems, or they may use the thermometers as number lines. Discuss how you might solve the first problem using addition and subtraction. (5 + 10 = 15. 15 − 5 = 10)
- When students have completed the activity, have them answer these questions.
- *On which day was the temperature coldest at 5:00?* (February 24)
- *On which day did the temperature drop the most between noon and 5:00?* (February 27)
- *On which day was the difference between the dawn temperature and the 5:00 temperature the greatest?* (February 26)

Name ______________________________

Same Shape

Circle the same shape.

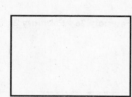

1.
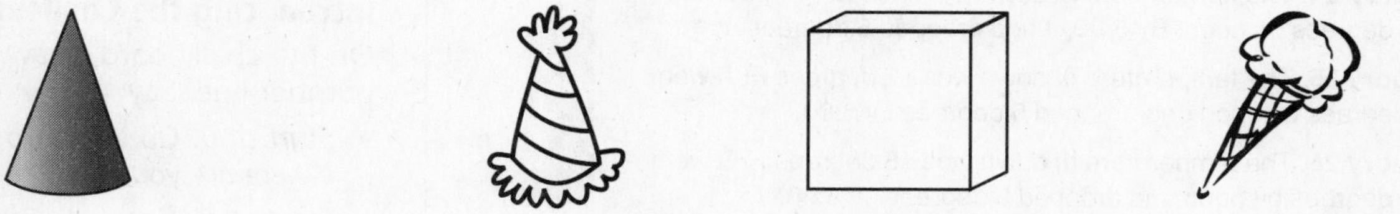

2.
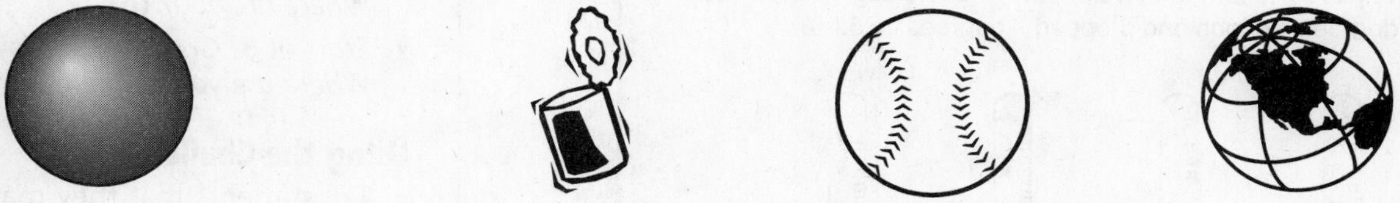

3.
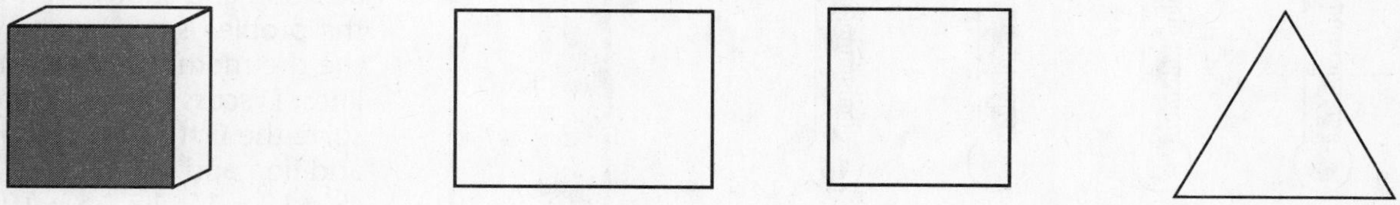

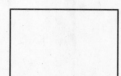

4.
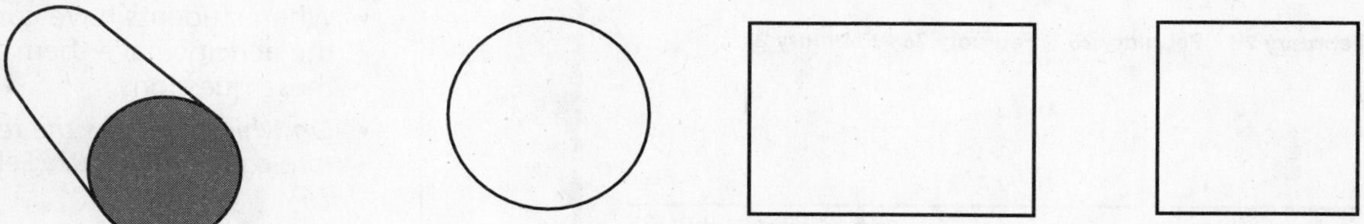

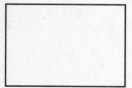

Sides and Corners

Write the number of sides. Write the number of corners.

5.
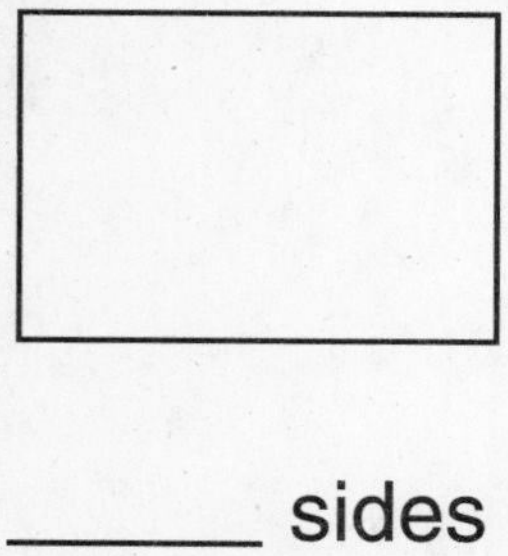

______ sides

______ corners

6.
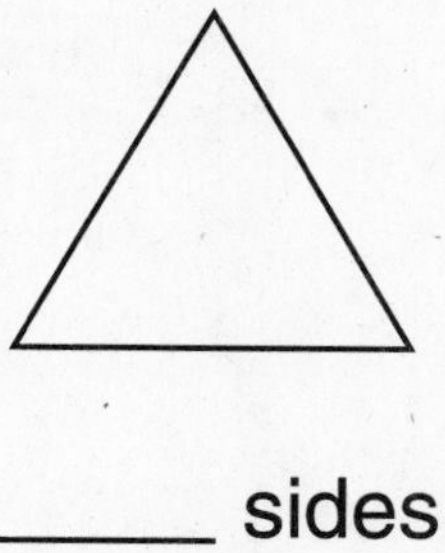

______ sides

______ corners

Equal Parts

Circle the shape that shows equal parts.

7.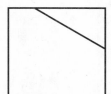

8.

Same Size and Shape

Circle the same size and shape.

9.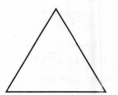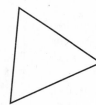

10.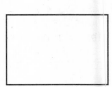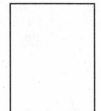

CHAPTER 10 PRE-CHAPTER ASSESSMENT

Assessment Goal

This two-page assessment covers skills identified as necessary for success in Chapter 10 Geometry. The first page assesses the major prerequisite skills for Cluster A. The second page assesses the major prerequisite skills for Cluster B. When the Cluster A and Cluster B prerequisite skills overlap, the skill(s) will be covered in only one section.

Getting Started

- Allow students time to look over the two pages of the assessment. Point out the labels that identify the skills covered.
- Have students find math vocabulary terms used in the assessment. List vocabulary terms on the board as students identify them. If necessary, review the meanings of all essential math vocabulary.

Introducing the Assessment

- Explain to students that these pages will help you know if they are ready to start a new chapter in their math textbooks.
- Students who have transferred from another school may not have been introduced to some of these skills. Encourage students to do their best and assure them you will help them learn any needed skills.

Cluster A Challenge

Those students who demonstrate mastery of the skills on this page will not need to use the reteaching worksheets. Instead, these students can do the Cluster A Challenge found on page 92.

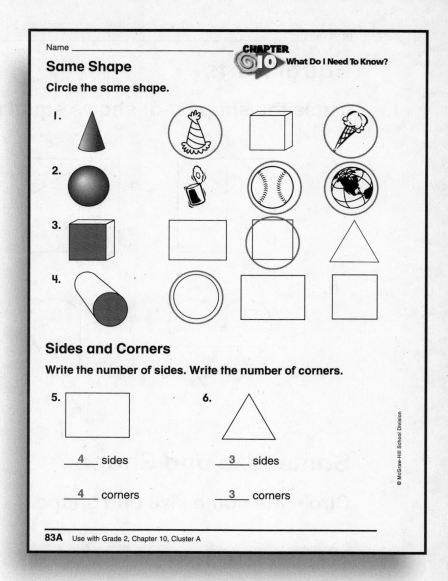

Name _____

Same Shape

Circle the same shape.

1.

2.

3.

4.

Sides and Corners

Write the number of sides. Write the number of corners.

5.

_4_ sides

_4_ corners

6.

_3_ sides

_3_ corners

© McGraw-Hill School Division

CLUSTER A PREREQUISITE SKILLS

The skills listed in this chart are those identified as major prerequisite skills for students' success in the lessons in Cluster A of the chapter. Each skill is covered by one or more assessment items as shown in the middle column. The right column provides the page numbers for the lessons in this book that reteach the Cluster A prerequisite skills.

Skill Name	Assessment Items	Lesson Pages
Same Shape	1-4	84-87
Sides and Corners	5-6	88

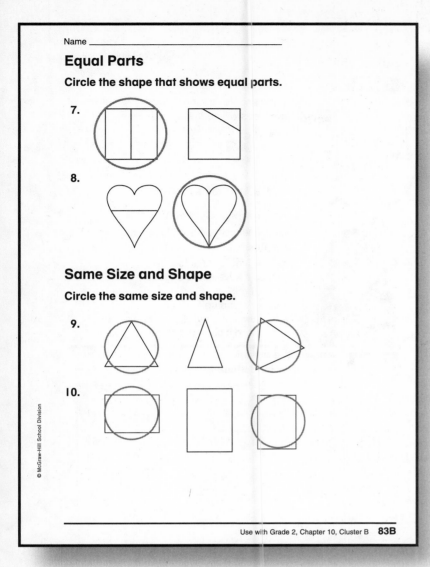

Name _____

Equal Parts

Circle the shape that shows equal parts.

7.

8.

Same Size and Shape

Circle the same size and shape.

9.

10.

Use with Grade 2, Chapter 10, Cluster B **83B**

CLUSTER B PREREQUISITE SKILLS

The skills listed in this chart are those identified as major prerequisite skills for students' success in the lessons in Cluster B of the chapter. Each skill is covered by one or more assessment items as shown in the middle column. The right column provides the page numbers for the lessons in this book that reteach the Cluster B prerequisite skills

Skill Name	Assessment Items	Lesson Pages
Equal Parts	7-8	89
Same Size and Shape	9-10	90-91

CHAPTER 10 PRE-CHAPTER ASSESSMENT

Alternative Assessment Strategies

- Oral administration of the assessment is appropriate for younger students or those whose native language is not English. Read the skills title and directions one section at a time. Check students' understanding by asking them to tell you how they will do the first exercise in the group.

- For some skill types you may wish to use group administration. In this technique, a small group or pair of students complete the assessment together. Through their discussion, you will be able to decide if supplementary reteaching materials are needed.

Intervention Materials

If students are not successful with the prerequisite skills assessed on these pages, reteaching lessons have been created to help them make the transition into the chapter.

Item correlation charts showing the skills lessons suitable for reteaching the prerequisite skills are found beneath the reproductions of each page of the assessment.

Cluster B Challenge

Those students who demonstrate mastery of the skills on this page will not need to use the reteaching worksheets. Instead, these students can do the Cluster B Challenge found on page 93.

Grade 2, Chapter 10, Cluster B **83D**

Lesson Goal

- Identify three-dimensional figures with the same shape.

What the Student Needs to Know

- Recognize two-dimensional shapes.
- Recognize attributes of shapes.

Getting Started

Display an attribute block triangle and a triangular prism. Ask:

- *How are these shapes different?* (One is flat, and the other is not.)
- *How are these shapes similar?* (They have three sides; the prism has faces that have three corners like those on the triangle.)

What Can I Do?

Read the question and the response. Then read and discuss the examples. Ask:

- *What flat faces appear on a cylinder?* (2 circles)
- *Which other shape has a flat face that is a circle?* (a cone)
- *Which shapes can roll?* (a cylinder, a cone, a sphere)

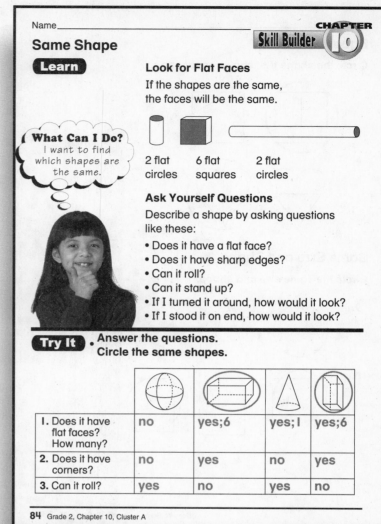

Name_____

Same Shape

Learn

Look for Flat Faces

If the shapes are the same, the faces will be the same.

2 flat circles   6 flat squares   2 flat circles

What Can I Do? I want to find which shapes are the same.

Ask Yourself Questions

Describe a shape by asking questions like these:

- Does it have a flat face?
- Does it have sharp edges?
- Can it roll?
- Can it stand up?
- If I turned it around, how would it look?
- If I stood it on end, how would it look?

Try It · Answer the questions. Circle the same shapes.

1. Does it have flat faces? How many?	no	yes;6	yes;1	yes;6
2. Does it have corners?	no	yes	no	yes
3. Can it roll?	yes	no	yes	no

© McGraw-Hill School Division

84 Grade 2, Chapter 10, Cluster A

WHAT IF THE STUDENT CAN'T

Recognize Two-Dimensional Shapes

- Distribute attribute blocks and have the student sort them into piles of triangles, rectangles, squares, and circles. Ask the student to tell how each kind of block differs from the others.

Recognize Attributes of Shapes

Distribute attribute blocks. Have the student sort them into the following groups:

- all the blocks that have straight edges
- all the blocks that are round
- all the blocks that have more than three sides

Power Practice • Circle the same shapes.

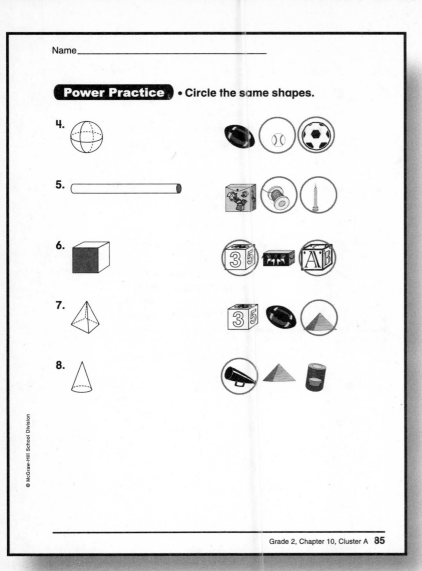

4.

5.

6.

7.

8.

USING THE LESSON

Try It

You may wish to use a wooden model to demonstrate how to count the faces of a rectangular prism. Remind students that once they have answered all the questions, they should circle the shapes that are the same.

Power Practice

- Tell students to refer to the list of questions on page 84 as they complete this exercise.
- Have students complete the practice items. Then review each answer.

Learn with Partners & Parents

Have students go on a Shape Hunt in the classroom or at home to find objects that have these shapes:

- sphere
- rectangular prism
- cone
- cylinder

Have students record the items they find and share their lists with the class.

WHAT IF THE STUDENT CAN'T

Complete the Power Practice

- Make sure the student can identify the pictured objects.
- Point out that each shape matches two of the pictured objects.

- Have the student explain what attributes the objects he or she circled have in common with the given shape.

Lesson Goal

- Identify the shape of a given face of a three-dimensional figure.

What the Student Needs to Know

- Trace around a solid.
- Recognize two-dimensional shapes.
- Recognize attributes of shapes.

Getting Started

- Display a small box. Then take it apart and display it as a flat surface. Have students point to the faces and identify them as rectangles or squares. Then refold the box to recreate the original figure.

What Can I Do?

Read the question and the response. Then read and discuss the examples. Display a triangular pyramid (all four faces triangles) and a cube and ask:

- *How are the faces of these shapes different?* (The faces of one are triangles; the faces of the other are squares.)

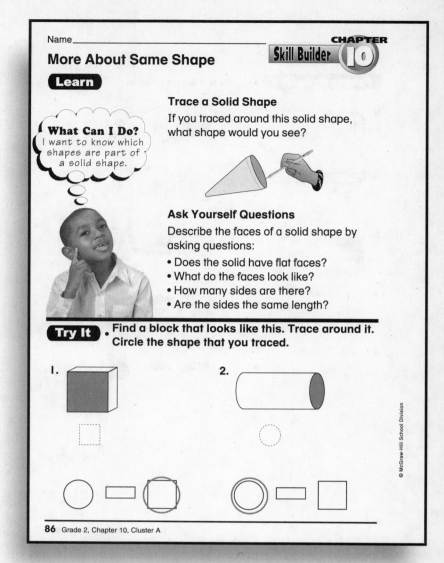

Name_____

Skill Builder CHAPTER 10

More About Same Shape

Learn

What Can I Do?
I want to know which shapes are part of a solid shape.

Trace a Solid Shape

If you traced around this solid shape, what shape would you see?

Ask Yourself Questions

Describe the faces of a solid shape by asking questions:

- Does the solid have flat faces?
- What do the faces look like?
- How many sides are there?
- Are the sides the same length?

Try It • Find a block that looks like this. Trace around it. Circle the shape that you traced.

1.

2.

© McGraw-Hill School Division

86 Grade 2, Chapter 10, Cluster A

WHAT IF THE STUDENT CAN'T

Trace Around a Solid

- Begin by having the student trace around attribute blocks. Once he or she is comfortable with that, provide solid figures. Demonstrate how to hold the figure still while you trace around the bottom of it.

Recognize Two-Dimensional Shapes

- Distribute a variety of attribute blocks and ask the student to find 2 rectangles, 3 squares, 1 circle, and 4 triangles.

Name_____

Power Practice • Circle the same shape.

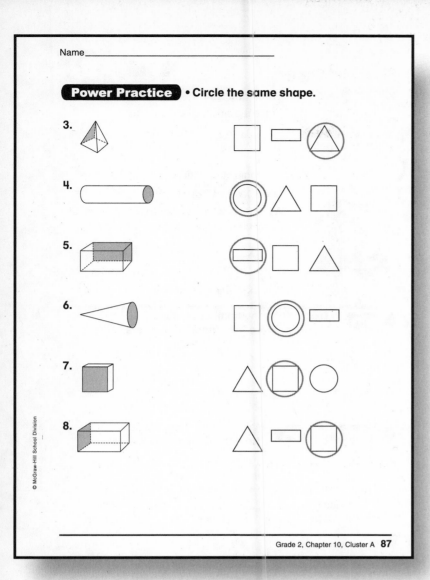

3.

4.

5.

6.

7.

8.

Try It

Provide cubes and cylinders for students to trace. Remind them to hold the figure still and trace around the bottom—the part that rests on the paper.

Power Practice

• Explain that instead of tracing the face on each solid figure, the artist has shaded the face. Students are to find the shape that matches the shaded face.

• Have students complete the practice items. Then review each answer.

WHAT IF THE STUDENT CAN'T

Recognize Attributes of Shapes

Distribute a variety of attribute blocks. Have the student sort them into the following groups:

• all the blocks that have three sides

• all the blocks that are round

• all the blocks that have sides the same length

Complete the Power Practice

• Have the student use solid figures to identify each solid figure that is pictured.

• Have the student name the shape of each of the three choices given for each exercise.

• Ask the student to match the shape to the face of the solid figure.

© McGraw-Hill School Division

Lesson Goal

- Identify the number of sides and corners in a two-dimensional shape.

What the Student Needs to Know

- Trace around a shape.
- Count corners and sides of a shape.

Getting Started

Draw a rectangle on the chalkboard. Ask:

- *Does this shape have sides? How can I find out the number of sides?* (count them)
- Demonstrate numbering the sides in clockwise order. Count as you write the numbers.
- Draw a square on the chalkboard and have a volunteer number the sides. Repeat with a triangle.

What Can I Do?

Read the question and the response. Then read and discuss the examples. Ask:

- *What is true about a triangle's sides and corners?* (There are the same number of sides as corners.)
- *Why might it be useful to make Xs on corners before counting?* (to make sure you count all the corners)

Try It

Remind students to trace around the object, number the sides, and make Xs on the corners before recording the answers.

Power Practice

- Tell students they may use either strategy to complete items 3–5.
- You may wish to identify item 3 as a parallelogram and item 5 as a pentagon.
- Have students complete the practice items. Then review each answer.

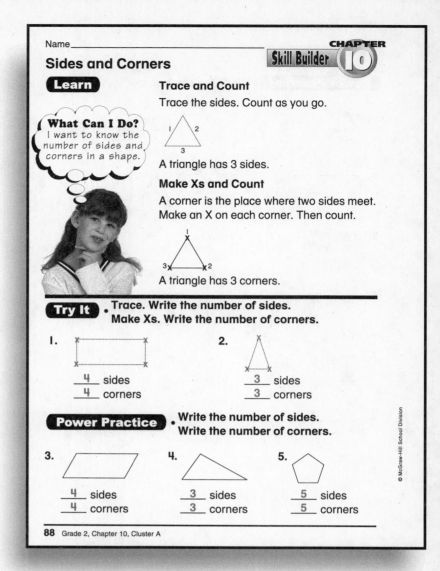

WHAT IF THE STUDENT CAN'T

Trace Around a Shape

- Have students practice tracing the letters of the alphabet on handwriting worksheets.
- Provide a variety of dotted shapes. Have the student demonstrate how to trace the shape. Show the student how to move around the shape without lifting the pencil.

Count Corners and Sides of a Shape

- Draw a shape on the chalkboard and number its corners clockwise. Have the student count the corners. Then ask the student to count the sides. Draw another shape on the chalkboard. This time, have the student number the corners.

Remind him or her to move around the shape in the same direction until all corners have been numbered. Then ask the student to count the sides.

Complete the Power Practice

- Have students count in front of you so you can make sure they are not omitting sides or corners as they count.

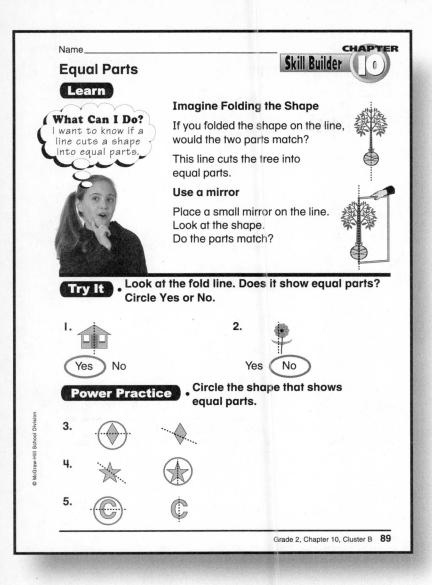

Equal Parts

Skill Builder CHAPTER 10

Learn

What Can I Do?
I want to know if a line cuts a shape into equal parts.

Imagine Folding the Shape

If you folded the shape on the line, would the two parts match?

This line cuts the tree into equal parts.

Use a mirror

Place a small mirror on the line.
Look at the shape.
Do the parts match?

Try It • Look at the fold line. Does it show equal parts?
Circle Yes or No.

1. (Yes) No

2. Yes (No)

Power Practice • Circle the shape that shows equal parts.

3.

4.

5.

© McGraw-Hill School Division

Grade 2, Chapter 10, Cluster B **89**

WHAT IF THE STUDENT CAN'T

Identify Matching Parts

- Fold a piece of construction paper and cut out a variety of shapes. Then cut the shapes apart on the fold. Mix up the pieces and have the student find the matching parts to make each whole shape.

Identify the Meaning of "Equal Parts"

- Cut out three equal-sized circles. Cut one in halves, one in fourths, and one in sixths. Have the student identify the number of equal parts in each circle.

- Cut out three equal-sized squares. Cut one in half vertically, one in half diagonally, and one in two unequal parts. Have the student identify the squares with equal parts.

Complete the Power Practice

- Discuss each incorrect answer. Have students trace the shape on tracing paper, cut it out, and fold it to test the symmetry.

USING THE LESSON

Lesson Goal
- Identify lines of symmetry.

What the Student Needs to Know
- Identify matching parts.
- Recognize the meaning of "equal parts."

Getting Started
Fold a piece of paper and cut out a heart shape. Open the paper again. Say:
- *This heart is made up of two equal parts.*

Fold the paper again and cut out a bow tie shape. Open the paper. Say:
- *This bow is made up of two equal parts.*

What Can I Do?
Read the question and the response. Then read and discuss the examples.
- Have a volunteer come to the chalkboard to draw a shape that could not be folded into two matching parts.
- Have another volunteer draw a shape that could be folded into two matching parts.
- Discuss the differences between the two shapes.

Try It
Remind students that equal parts need not face the same way. However, when the shape is folded, the parts must match.

Power Practice
- Have students complete the practice items. Then review each answer.

Lesson Goal
- Identify congruent figures.

What the Student Needs to Know
- Recognize turns.
- Trace around a shape.

Getting Started
Cut out a large cardboard triangle. On the chalkboard, trace around the triangle with colored chalk. Then turn it and trace it again. Ask:

- *How do you know that these are the same shape? the same size?* (You traced the same triangle.)
- *How else could you tell that these are the same size and shape?* (Measure them; trace one shape and place it over the other.)

What Can I Do?
Read the question and the response. Then read and discuss the examples. Ask:

- *Can two figures be the same shape but not the same size?* (yes) *the same size but not the same shape?* (yes)
- *When might you need to know whether two figures are the same size and shape?* (when you are building or making something)

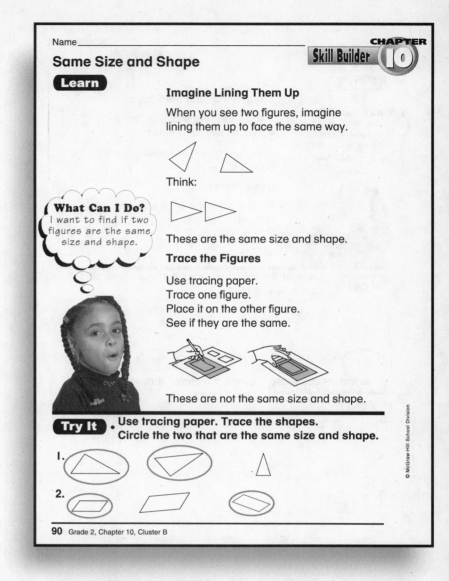

Name _____

Same Size and Shape

Learn

Imagine Lining Them Up
When you see two figures, imagine lining them up to face the same way.

Think:

These are the same size and shape.

Trace the Figures
Use tracing paper.
Trace one figure.
Place it on the other figure.
See if they are the same.

These are not the same size and shape.

What Can I Do?
I want to find if two figures are the same size and shape.

Try It Use tracing paper. Trace the shapes. Circle the two that are the same size and shape.

1.

2.

© McGraw-Hill School Division

90 Grade 2, Chapter 10, Cluster B

WHAT IF THE STUDENT CAN'T

Recognize Turns
- Fold a piece of construction paper in quarters and draw a shape. Have the student cut out the shape and then paste all four shapes in different configurations on another sheet of paper.

- Place an attribute block on an index card and trace around it. Turn the block 90 degrees and trace it again on another card. Repeat with other blocks. Mix up the cards and have the student identify the matching shapes.

Name_____

Power Practice • Circle the two that are the same size and shape.

3.

4.

5.

6.

7.

8.

© McGraw-Hill School Division

Grade 2, Chapter 10, Cluster B **91**

Try It

• Provide tracing paper. If necessary, demonstrate how to use it.

• Remind students to circle the two that are the same size and shape after they trace and compare.

Power Practice

• Students may use tracing paper if they wish.

• Have students complete the practice items. Then discuss their answers.

WHAT IF THE STUDENT CAN'T

Trace Around a Shape

• Provide attribute blocks. Have the student practice tracing each shape. Then have the student use scissors to cut around the shape he or she traced.

Complete the Power Practice

• Review all the choices, having the student identify each figure in relation to the first figure. For example, for item 3, the student might say, "Circle, not a circle, bigger circle, same size and shape circle." For item 4, he or she might say, "Triangle, smaller triangle, same size and shape triangle, different shaped triangle."

Lesson Goal
- Draw lines to divide figures into given shapes.

Introducing the Challenge
On the chalkboard, draw an 18"-x-9" rectangle. Say:

- *With 1 line, I can make this into 2 squares.*

Draw a line down the middle of the rectangle to divide it into squares. Then erase the line. Say:

- *With 2 lines, I can make this into 4 rectangles.*

Draw intersecting lines to make the rectangle into four rectangles. Then erase the lines. Say:

- *How could I draw 2 lines to make this into 3 rectangles?*

Allow volunteers to try. (Draw two lines parallel to any side.)

Using the Challenge
- Read each direction line aloud. Tell the students that there may be more than one way to solve each problem.
- Suggest that students first draw their answers lightly in pencil so that they can erase if they are incorrect.
- When everyone has finished, have volunteers draw their solutions on the chalkboard.

Make New Shapes

Look at each shape.
Follow the directions. Answers may vary.

Draw 1 line to make 2 smaller triangles.

Draw 1 line to make 2 rectangles.

Draw 1 line to make 2 triangles.

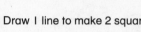

Draw 1 line to make 2 squares.

Draw 3 lines to make 1 square and 3 smaller triangles.

Draw 3 lines to make 4 smaller triangles.

© McGraw-Hill School Division

Name_____

Symmetrical Numerals

There are two ways to show that each of these numbers has equal parts.

If you fold these numbers along either line, the parts will match.

  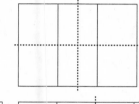

Write numbers that have matching parts. Draw lines to show the matching parts. You may use these grids to help you. Possible answers include 0, 1, and 8 written in any combination. For example: 101, 111, 818, 888, 1111, 8008, 8118, and 8888.

Grade 2, Chapter 10, Cluster B **93**

CHALLENGE

Lesson Goal
- Identify lines of symmetry.

Introducing the Challenge
- Demonstrate lines of symmetry using a cut-paper M (fold down the center), C (fold across the middle), and Q (no line of symmetry is possible). Then show that with letter O, there is more than one line of symmetry (down the center and across the middle, for example).

Using the Challenge
- Review the information at the top of the worksheet. If you wish, demonstrate the lines of symmetry with a cut-paper 0, 1, and 8.
- When students have completed the activity, have them share their answers with the class.

Equal Parts

Write the number of equal parts.

1.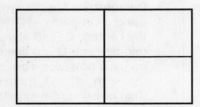

_____ equal parts

2.

_____ equal parts

Greater Than and Less Than

Compare. Write >, < or =.

3. 4 _____ 5

4. 8 _____ 6

5. 3 _____ 4

Parts of a Group

Write how many.

6. How many As? _____

7. How many Bs? _____

8. How many in all? _____

Certain, Maybe, Impossible

Will it happen?
Circle certain, maybe, or impossible.

9. You pick a .

certain

maybe

impossible

10. You pick a .

certain

maybe

impossible

Assessment Goal

This two-page assessment covers skills identified as necessary for success in Chapter 11 Fractions and Probability. The first page assesses the major prerequisite skills for Cluster A. The second page assesses the major prerequisite skills for Cluster B. When the Cluster A and Cluster B prerequisite skills overlap, the skill(s) will be covered in only one section.

Getting Started

- Allow students time to look over the two pages of the assessment. Point out the labels that identify the skills covered.

- Have students find math vocabulary terms used in the assessment. List vocabulary terms on the board as students identify them. If necessary, review the meanings of all essential math vocabulary.

Introducing the Assessment

- Explain to students that these pages will help you know if they are ready to start a new chapter in their math textbooks.

- Students who have transferred from another school may not have been introduced to some of these skills. Encourage students to do their best and assure them you will help them learn any needed skills.

Cluster A Challenge

Those students who demonstrate mastery of the skills on this page will not need to use the reteaching worksheets. Instead, these students can do the Cluster A Challenge found on page 100.

Name_____

Equal Parts

Write the number of equal parts.

I.

2.

__4__ equal parts   __6__ equal parts

Greater Than and Less Than

Compare. Write >, < or =.

3. 4 __<__ 5

4. 8 __>__ 6

5. 3 __<__ 4

CLUSTER A PREREQUISITE SKILLS

The skills listed in this chart are those identified as major prerequisite skills for students' success in the lessons in Cluster A of the chapter. Each skill is covered by one or more assessment items as shown in the middle column. The right column provides the page numbers for the lessons in this book that reteach the Cluster A prerequisite skills.

Skill Name	Assessment Items	Lesson Pages
Equal Parts	1-2	94-95
Greater Than and Less Than	3-5	96

Name_____

Parts of a Group

Write how many.

Ⓐ Ⓐ Ⓐ Ⓐ Ⓑ Ⓑ Ⓑ Ⓒ

6. How many As? _____4_____

7. How many Bs? _____3_____

8. How many in all? _____8_____

Certain, Maybe, Impossible

Will it happen?
Circle certain, maybe, or impossible.

9. You pick a Ⓑ.

certain

(maybe)

impossible

10. You pick a Ⓒ.

certain

maybe

(impossible)

© McGraw-Hill School Division

CLUSTER B PREREQUISITE SKILLS

The skills listed in this chart are those identified as major prerequisite skills for students' success in the lessons in Cluster B of the chapter. Each skill is covered by one or more assessment items as shown in the middle column. The right column provides the page numbers for the lessons in this book that reteach the Cluster B prerequisite skills

Skill Name	Assessment Items	Lesson Pages
Parts of a Group	6-8	97
Certain, Maybe, Impossible	9-10	98-99

Alternative Assessment Strategies

- Oral administration of the assessment is appropriate for younger students or those whose native language is not English. Read the skills title and directions one section at a time. Check students' understanding by asking them to tell you how they will do the first exercise in the group.

- For some skill types you may wish to use group administration. In this technique, a small group or pair of students complete the assessment together. Through their discussion, you will be able to decide if supplementary reteaching materials are needed.

Intervention Materials

If students are not successful with the prerequisite skills assessed on these pages, reteaching lessons have been created to help them make the transition into the chapter.

Item correlation charts showing the skills lessons suitable for reteaching the prerequisite skills are found beneath the reproductions of each page of the assessment.

Cluster B Challenge

Those students who demonstrate mastery of the skills on this page will not need to use the reteaching worksheets. Instead, these students can do the Cluster B Challenge found on page 101.

Lesson Goal

• Identify equal parts of a figure.

What the Student Needs to Know

• Count parts of a shape.

• Recognize the meaning of "equal parts."

Getting Started

Fold a piece of paper in half and then in half again. Open it. Ask:

• *How many parts did I make?* (4)

Fold the paper again and hold it up. Ask:

• *How can you tell that the parts are equal?* (They match when they are placed on top of each other.)

What Can I Do?

Read the question and the response. Then read and discuss the examples. Ask:

• *What is the difference between equal parts and parts that are not equal?* (Equal parts are the same size and shape. Parts that are not equal are not the same size and shape.)

• Draw squares on the chalkboard. Have volunteers draw lines to divide the squares into equal parts. Discuss different ways of making equal parts.

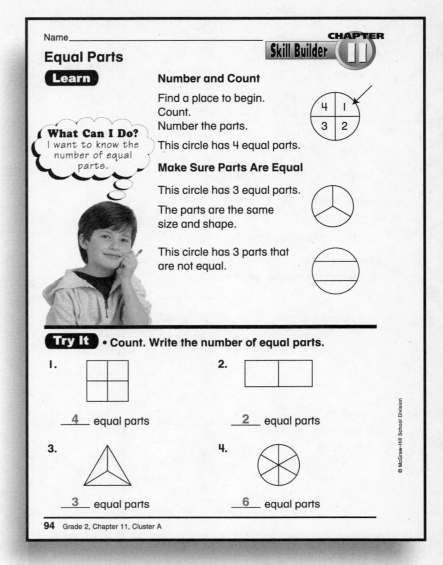

WHAT IF THE STUDENT CAN'T

Count Parts of a Shape

• Draw several shapes on the chalkboard and divide them into two, four, and six equal parts. Number the parts and have the student count them. Then ask the student to number the parts of other shapes that you draw on the chalkboard. Remind the student to move around or across the shape in the same direction until all parts have been numbered.

Recognize the Meaning of "Equal Parts"

• Cut out a cardboard circle with a diameter equal to the length of a coffee stirrer or a similar object. Provide coffee stirrers and have the student use them to show how to divide the circle into 2 equal parts, 4 equal parts, and 6 equal parts.

Name_____

5.

__2__ equal parts

6.

__3__ equal parts

7.

__6__ equal parts

8.

__2__ equal parts

9.

__4__ equal parts

10.

__3__ equal parts

11.

__2__ equal parts

12.

__6__ equal parts

13.

__4__ equal parts

14.

__3__ equal parts

© McGraw-Hill School Division

Grade 2, Chapter 11, Cluster A **95**

Try It

Remind students that they are to count the parts, numbering them as they go, before writing the total number of equal parts.

Power Practice

- Have students complete the practice items. Then review each answer.
- Discuss how students know that the parts shown are equal. (They are the same size and shape.)

WHAT IF THE STUDENT CAN'T

- Cut out three equal-sized rectangles. Cut one in half vertically, one in half horizontally, and one in two unequal parts. Have the student identify the rectangles with equal parts.

Complete the Power Practice
- Discuss each incorrect answer. Have the student number the parts of the shape before counting them aloud.

Lesson Goal
• Compare numbers using the symbols >, <, and =.

What the Student Needs to Know
• Recognize the meaning of *greater than, less than, and equal.*
• Read a number line.

Getting Started
Cut out a large tagboard > sign. On the chalkboard, write the following number pairs:
• 11   18
• 7   16
• 14   13

Have volunteers come to the chalkboard and point to the lesser number in the pair. Then have them point to the greater number in the pair. Help students to say which number is less than the other and which is greater.

What Can I Do?
Read the question and the response. Then read and discuss the examples. Ask:
• *What's an easy way to remember which way to point the "greater than" symbol?* (Always point to the smaller number.)
• *If number A is to the left of number B on a number line, which number is less?* (number A)

Try It
Remind students to first locate the numbers on the number line and then compare.

Power Practice
• Have students complete the practice items. Then review each answer. Discuss the strategies students used to compare the numbers.

Name_____

Greater Than and Less Than

Learn

What Can I Do?
I want to compare two numbers using >, <, or =.

Understand the Symbols

The symbol > means "greater than."
The open side of the symbol is next to the greater number.

    5 > 3 means 5 is greater than 3.

The symbol < means "less than."
The symbol points to the smaller number.

    3 < 5 means 3 is less than 5.

Use a Number Line

Greater numbers are always on the right.
Lesser numbers are always on the left.

    0 1 2 3 4 5 6 7 8 9 10

Think: 5 is to the right of 3, so 5 > 3.

Try It • Use the number line. Compare. Write >, <, or =.

    0 1 2 3 4 5 6 7 8 9 10

1. 6 $<$ 7   2. 3 $=$ 3   3. 8 $<$ 10

Power Practice • Compare. Write >, <, or =.

4. 12 $>$ 10   6. 5 $=$ 5

5. 6 $<$ 16   7. 15 $<$ 16

WHAT IF THE STUDENT CAN'T

Recognize the Meaning of *Greater Than, Less Than,* and *Equal*

• On the chalkboard, write 8 and 12. Ask: *Which number is greater?* (12) *Which number is less?* (8)
• Then write these sentences on the chalkboard:
  __ is less than __.
  __ is greater than __.
  Ask students to complete each sentence using the numbers 8 and 12.
• Do the same for other number pairs from 1–20.

Read a Number Line
On the board, draw a 0–10 number line. Ask the student:
• *Which numbers are less than 6?* (0, 1, . . .5)
• *Which numbers are greater than 3?* (4, 5, 6,. . .10)
• *Which numbers are less than 4?* (0, 1, 2, 3)
• *Which numbers are greater than 7?* (8, 9, 10)

Complete the Power Practice
• Discuss each incorrect answer. Draw a 0–20 number line and have the student use it to compare the numbers.

Name_____

Parts of a Group

 Skill Builder

Learn

What Can I Do?
I want to know how many objects are in one part of a group.

Find the Parts

This group has different parts.

2 buttons are large and white.
3 buttons are small and black.
1 button is fancy and gray.

There are 3 different kinds of buttons.
There are 3 parts of the group.

Count, Circle, Count

Count how many in all.
Circle the ones that belong together.
Count the objects in each circle.

Try It • Count, circle, and count. Write how many.

1. How many in all? __8__   2. How many ? __2__

Power Practice • Write how many.

Z	X	W	Z	Y	X	Z	Z	X	Z	Y	Z

3. How many in all? __12__   4. How many Xs? __3__

5. How many Zs? __6__   6. How many Ws? __1__

Grade 2, Chapter 11, Cluster B   **97**

WHAT IF THE STUDENT CAN'T

Recognize Differences
• Give the student the following attribute blocks: 2 red squares, 2 red circles. Have the student identify what is different about the pairs. (shape) Continue with 2 large red squares and 2 small red squares. (size) Continue with 2 large red squares and 2 small red circles. (size and shape)

Count Parts of a Group
• Distribute large attribute blocks that are the same shape but of 3 different colors. Have the student sort the blocks into groups and count the members of each group. Repeat with a different number of blocks.

Complete the Power Practice
• Review any incorrect answers. Have the student use the Count, Circle, Count strategy when necessary.

USING THE LESSON

Lesson Goal
• Identify parts of a group.

What the Student Needs to Know
• Recognize differences.
• Count parts of a group.

Getting Started
Display 6 attribute blocks—3 large yellow circles and 3 large red circles. Ask:
• *How many circles are there?* (6)
• *How are the circles different?* (They are different colors.)
• *How many different colors do you see?* (2) So this group of circles has 2 parts—red circles and yellow circles.

What Can I Do?
Read the question and the response. Then read and discuss the examples. Ask:
• *How can you decide which buttons belong together?* (Look for the buttons with the same size, shape, and color.)
• *Can the parts of a group have different numbers of items?* (yes)

Try It
Have students follow these steps:
• Count how many buttons there are in all.
• Circle the buttons that belong together.
• Count how many buttons are gray.

Power Practice
• Have students complete the practice items. Then review each answer.

Lesson Goal

- Identify the likelihood of an event.

What the Student Needs to Know

- Recognize the meaning of "possible" and "impossible."
- Recognize coins.

Getting Started

Place a red crayon and a blue crayon in a paper bag. Ask:

- *If you put your hand in the bag, could you pick out a red crayon? (yes) We say that it is "possible" to pick a red crayon.*
- *If you put your hand in, could you pick out a yellow crayon? (no) Why not? (There are no yellow crayons in the bag.) We say that it is "impossible" to pick a yellow crayon.*

What Can I Do?

Read the question and the response. Then read and discuss the examples. Ask:

- *Suppose there were 5 nickels instead of 5 pennies. Which pick would be certain? (picking a nickel)*
- *Which picks would be impossible? (Possible answer: picking a penny, dime, or quarter)*
- *Would any picks be "maybes"? (no)*

Name_____

Certain, Maybe, Impossible

Learn

Is It Possible?

Is it possible to pick a quarter?
Is it possible to pick a nickel?

Think: There are no quarters.
So, picking a quarter is impossible.
There are no nickels.
So, picking a nickel is impossible.

Decide Between Certain and Maybe

What Can I Do?
I want to know if something could happen or could not happen.

If you pick one coin, what could it be?

Think: All the coins are pennies.
So, picking a penny is certain.

If you pick one coin, what could it be?

Think: Some coins are pennies.
Picking a penny could happen.
Some coins are dimes.
Picking a dime could happen.
So, picking a penny and picking a dime are both "maybes."

© McGraw-Hill School Division

WHAT IF THE STUDENT CAN'T

Recognize the Meanings of "Possible" and "Impossible"

Have the student identify the following occurrences as being possible or impossible.

- A squirrel eats a nut.
- A squirrel flies a plane.
- A cloud floats overhead.
- A cloud speaks aloud.

Ask the student to give other examples of possible and impossible events.

Recognize Coins

- Display a play penny, nickel, dime, and quarter. Remove one of the coins and have the student tell which coin is missing and what its value is.

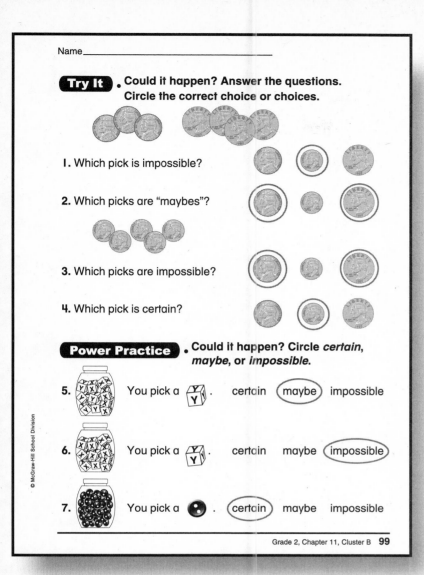

Name_____

Try It . Could it happen? Answer the questions.
Circle the correct choice or choices.

1. Which pick is impossible?

2. Which picks are "maybes"?

3. Which picks are impossible?

4. Which pick is certain?

Power Practice . Could it happen? Circle *certain*,
maybe, or *impossible*.

5. You pick a (Y/Y die). certain (maybe) impossible

6. You pick a (Y/Y die). certain maybe (impossible)

7. You pick a ●. (certain) maybe impossible

© McGraw-Hill School Division

Try It
- Point out that students may circle more than one coin in each group.
- If you wish, demonstrate each exercise, using 3 play nickels, 4 play quarters, 5 play dimes, and a paper bag.

Power Practice
- Have students complete the practice items. Then discuss their answers. Have students explain their reasoning.
- If you wish, demonstrate each exercise, using play money, alphabet blocks, and buttons.

Learn with Partners & Parents
Give students hands-on experience with probability with this sock-matching activity.
- Put 3 white socks and 3 blue socks in a bag (or any other color). Have the student decide whether picking a white sock is certain, a maybe, or impossible. (a maybe)
- Repeat with 2 white socks and 4 blue socks (maybe), 6 white socks (certain), and 6 blue socks (impossible).

WHAT IF THE STUDENT CAN'T

Complete the Power Practice
- For each item, have the student identify the possible choices, the pick shown, and then explain why that pick is certain, maybe, or impossible. If necessary, act out each exercise using manipulatives.

CHALLENGE

Lesson Goal
- Use pictures to add and subtract fractions.

Introducing the Challenge
On the chalkboard, draw a circle. Divide it in fourths. Say:
- *I ate $\frac{1}{4}$ of this muffin.*

Shade $\frac{1}{4}$ of the circle. Ask:
- *How can I tell what fraction of the muffin is left?* (Count the fourths that are left.)
- *What fraction of the muffin is left?* ($\frac{3}{4}$)

Using the Challenge
- Make sure each student has a red, blue, and green crayon. Read the directions aloud.
- When everyone has finished, discuss the strategies students used to find the answers. Talk about whether it makes more sense to color the parts in a certain order or to color them in random order.

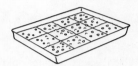

CHALLENGE **CHAPTER 11**

Adding and Subtracting Fractions

Use red, blue, and green crayons.
Color the fractions.
Solve the problems.

Molly = Color it red.
Sally = Color it blue.
Billy = Color it green.

Molly ate $\frac{1}{8}$.

Sally ate $\frac{2}{8}$.

Billy ate $\frac{3}{8}$.

What fraction is left? $\frac{2}{8}$

(or $\frac{1}{4}$)

Molly ate $\frac{3}{12}$.

Sally ate $\frac{4}{12}$.

Billy ate $\frac{1}{12}$.

What fraction is left? $\frac{4}{12}$

(or $\frac{1}{3}$)

Molly ate $\frac{1}{4}$.

Sally ate $\frac{2}{4}$.

Billy ate $\frac{1}{4}$.

What fraction is left? $\frac{0}{4}$

(or 0)

Name_____

Number Experiment

You will need a paper bag and six tagboard strips.
Write each of these numbers on a strip:

| 3 | 7 | 11 | 24 | 48 | 100 |

Put the strips in the bag.

Which kind of number will you pick most often?
Circle your guess.

one-digit number   two-digit number   three-digit number

1. Shake the bag.
2. Pick a number.
3. Make a tally mark on the chart.
4. Put the number back.

Do this 20 times in all. Was your guess correct?

Number	Tally
3	
7	
11	
24	
48	
100	

Guesses may vary. The best guess is "2-digit number",
because half of the numbers are 2-digit numbers,
$\frac{1}{3}$ are 1-digit numbers, and $\frac{1}{6}$ are 3-digit numbers.
Results will vary.

Lesson Goal

• Identify the likeliest outcome.

Introducing the Challenge

• Have students give examples of 1-digit, 2-digit, and 3-digit numbers. Write the numbers on the chalkboard as they are mentioned.

• Ask students to identify which kind of number was named most often, and which was named least often.

Using the Challenge

• Provide each group with a paper bag and six tagboard strips. Have them follow the directions and write the numbers, one on each strip, and then put the strips in the bag.

• Before students continue the experiment, make sure that each student circles his or her guess on the worksheet.

• When students have completed the activity, have them share their answers with the class. Discuss how they arrived at their original guess and whether or not their guess proved to be correct.

Numbers to 100

Write how many.

1.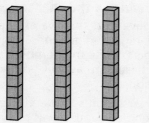

2.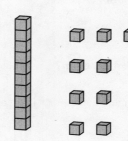

_____   _____

Tens and Ones

Write the number.

3.

tens	ones
7	4

4.

tens	ones
2	9

_____   _____

Number Patterns

Find the missing numbers in each counting pattern.

5. 6, 7, _____, 9, _____ 11, 12

6. 4, 14, _____, 34, 44, _____

Compare Numbers

Compare. Write >, <, or =.

7. 38 _____ 83

8. 26 _____ 25

Order Numbers

Write the number that comes just before.

9. _____ 76

Write the number that comes between.

10. 49 _____ 51

Assessment Goal

This two-page assessment covers skills identified as necessary for success in Chapter 12 Place Value to 1,000. The first page assesses the major prerequisite skills for Cluster A. The second page assesses the major prerequisite skills for Cluster B. When the Cluster A and Cluster B prerequisite skills overlap, the skill(s) will be covered in only one section.

Getting Started

- Allow students time to look over the two pages of the assessment. Point out the labels that identify the skills covered.
- Have students find math vocabulary terms used in the assessment. List vocabulary terms on the board as students identify them. If necessary, review the meanings of all essential math vocabulary.

Introducing the Assessment

- Explain to students that these pages will help you know if they are ready to start a new chapter in their math textbooks.
- Students who have transferred from another school may not have been introduced to some of these skills. Encourage students to do their best and assure them you will help them learn any needed skills.

Cluster A Challenge

Those students who demonstrate mastery of the skills on this page will not need to use the reteaching worksheets. Instead, these students can do the Cluster A Challenge found on page 112.

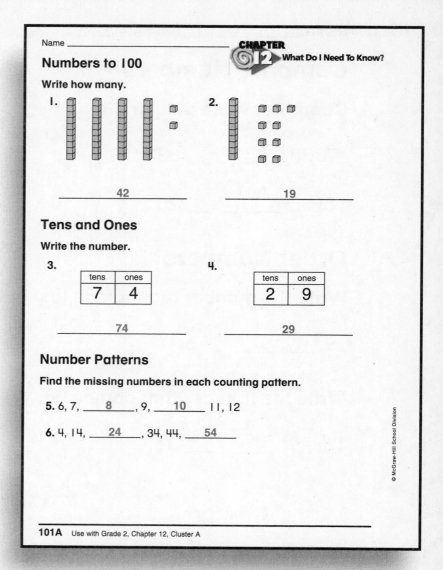

Name _____

CHAPTER 12 What Do I Need To Know?

Numbers to 100

Write how many.

1. _____42_____

2. _____19_____

Tens and Ones

Write the number.

3.
tens	ones
7	4

_____74_____

4.
tens	ones
2	9

_____29_____

Number Patterns

Find the missing numbers in each counting pattern.

5. 6, 7, ___8___, 9, ___10___ 11, 12

6. 4, 14, ___24___, 34, 44, ___54___

© McGraw-Hill School Division

101A Use with Grade 2, Chapter 12, Cluster A

CLUSTER A PREREQUISITE SKILLS

The skills listed in this chart are those identified as major prerequisite skills for students' success in the lessons in Cluster A of the chapter. Each skill is covered by one or more assessment items as shown in the middle column. The right column provides the page numbers for the lessons in this book that reteach the Cluster A prerequisite skills.

Skill Name	Assessment Items	Lesson Pages
Numbers to 100	1-2	102-103
Tens and Ones	3-4	104-105
Number Patterns	5-6	106-107

Name _____

Compare Numbers

Compare. Write >, <, or =.

7. 38 ___<___ 83

8. 26 ___>___ 25

Order Numbers

Write the number that comes just before.

9. ___75___ 76

Write the number that comes between.

10. 49 ___50___ 51

CLUSTER B PREREQUISITE SKILLS

The skills listed in this chart are those identified as major prerequisite skills for students' success in the lessons in Cluster B of the chapter. Each skill is covered by one or more assessment items as shown in the middle column. The right column provides the page numbers for the lessons in this book that reteach the Cluster B prerequisite skills

Skill Name	Assessment Items	Lesson Pages
Compare Numbers	7-8	108-109
Order Numbers	9-10	110-111

Alternative Assessment Strategies

- Oral administration of the assessment is appropriate for younger students or those whose native language is not English. Read the skills title and directions one section at a time. Check students' understanding by asking them to tell you how they will do the first exercise in the group.

- For some skill types you may wish to use group administration. In this technique, a small group or pair of students complete the assessment together. Through their discussion, you will be able to decide if supplementary reteaching materials are needed.

Intervention Materials

If students are not successful with the prerequisite skills assessed on these pages, reteaching lessons have been created to help them make the transition into the chapter.

Item correlation charts showing the skills lessons suitable for reteaching the prerequisite skills are found beneath the reproductions of each page of the assessment.

Cluster B Challenge

Those students who demonstrate mastery of the skills on this page will not need to use the reteaching worksheets. Instead, these students can do the Cluster B Challenge found on page 113.

Lesson Goal
- Write numbers to 100.

What the Student Needs to Know
- Count by 10s.
- Use place-value models.
- Read a place-value chart.

Getting Started
- Give pairs of students a handful of tens blocks. Have them count the blocks by 10s to find how many they have in all.

What Can I Do?
Read the question and the response. Then read and discuss the examples. Ask:

- *How would you skip count by 10s and count on to reach the number 43?* (10, 20, 30, 40; 41, 42, 43) *the number 51?* (10, 20, 30, 40, 50; 51)

- *In the number 54, which number shows the tens?* (5) *the ones?* (4)

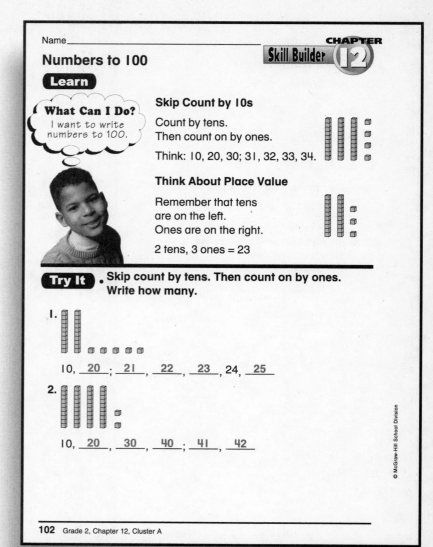

Name_____

Numbers to 100

Learn

What Can I Do?
I want to write numbers to 100.

Skip Count by 10s
Count by tens.
Then count on by ones.

Think: 10, 20, 30; 31, 32, 33, 34.

Think About Place Value
Remember that tens are on the left.
Ones are on the right.

2 tens, 3 ones = 23

Try It • Skip count by tens. Then count on by ones. Write how many.

1.

10, __20__ ; __21__ , __22__ , __23__ , 24, __25__

2.

10, __20__ , __30__ , __40__ ; __41__ , __42__

© McGraw-Hill School Division

WHAT IF THE STUDENT CAN'T

Count by 10s
- Provide a hundred chart and have the student read the numbers in the last column. Cover some of those numbers and have the student recite them again.

Use Place-Value Models
- Give the student 5 tens models and 5 ones models. Have the student show the numbers 4, 14, 24, 34, 44, and 54. Then have the student show 8, 12, 25, 31, 45, and 53.

Name _____

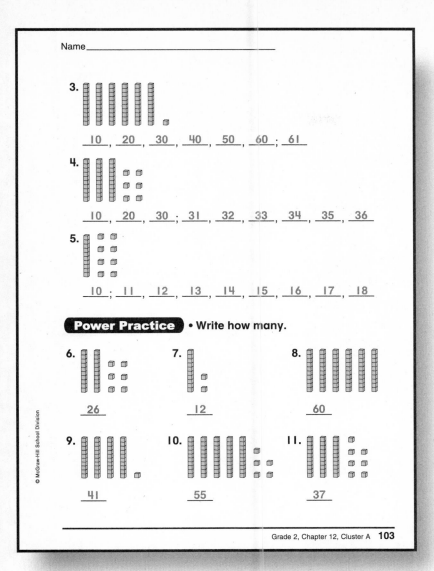

3.
   10 , 20 , 30 , 40 , 50 , 60 ; 61

4.
   10 , 20 , 30 ; 31 , 32 , 33 , 34 , 35 , 36

5.
   10 ; 11 , 12 , 13 , 14 , 15 , 16 , 17 , 18

Power Practice • Write how many.

6.   26

7.   12

8.   60

9.   41

10.   55

11.   37

© McGraw-Hill School Division

Try It

• Some students might benefit from using real tens and ones models to show each number.

• Remind students to count the tens models first and then count on with the ones models to find the number.

Power Practice

• Have students complete the practice items. Discuss their answers and the strategy they used to find them.

• Point out that 2 tens 6 ones is the same as 20 + 6; 1 ten 2 ones is the same as 10 + 2, and so on.

WHAT IF THE STUDENT CAN'T

Read a Place-Value Chart

• Have the student use some of the models from the activity above to show the numbers, and then write the numbers in a place-value chart. Ask the student to read the numbers aloud and identify the number of tens and ones.

Complete the Power Practice

• Discuss each incorrect answer. Have the student show each number with tens and ones models. Watch as he or she counts by 10s and then counts on to form the number.

Lesson Goal

- Write 2-digit numbers.

What the Student Needs to Know

- Identify place value.
- Count ten items.

Getting Started

Display 3 tens models and 3 ones models. Ask:

- *How can I use these models to show the number 21?* (2 tens models,1 ones model)
- *How many tens are in 21?* (2) *How many ones are in 21?* (1)

Repeat with the numbers 13 and 30.

What Can I Do?

Read the question and the response. Then read and discuss the examples. Ask:

- *What number has 4 tens and 2 ones?* (42) *2 tens and 4 ones?* (24) *1 ten and 6 ones?* (16) *6 tens and 1 one?* (61)
- *What is the greatest number you can make that has only two digits?* (99)

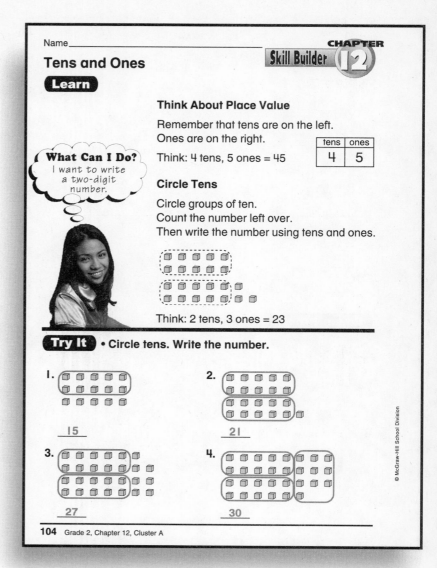

Name_____

Tens and Ones

Learn

What Can I Do?
I want to write a two-digit number.

Think About Place Value

Remember that tens are on the left.
Ones are on the right.

tens	ones
4	5

Think: 4 tens, 5 ones = 45

Circle Tens

Circle groups of ten.
Count the number left over.
Then write the number using tens and ones.

Think: 2 tens, 3 ones = 23

Try It • Circle tens. Write the number.

1.   15

2.   21

3.   27

4.   30

© McGraw-Hill School Division

104   Grade 2, Chapter 12, Cluster A

WHAT IF THE STUDENT CAN'T

Identify Place Value

- Draw a large place-value chart on the chalkboard. Write a variety of 2-digit numbers on index cards. Have the student draw cards and write the numbers in the place-value chart. Then ask the student to identify how many tens and ones are in each number.

Count Ten Items

- Give the student a pile of 15 counters and a large rubber band. Have the student count and use the rubber band to circle 10 counters. Mix the counters and have the student try again.

Name_____

5.
tens	ones
4	6

46

6.
tens	ones
7	2

72

7.
tens	ones
8	3

83

8.
tens	ones
3	5

35

9.
tens	ones
5	1

51

10.
tens	ones
1	7

17

11.
tens	ones
2	9

29

12.
tens	ones
6	7

67

13.
tens	ones
9	8

98

14.
tens	ones
2	4

24

© McGraw-Hill School Division

USING THE LESSON

Try It
Remind students to circle groups of ten ones models and count the ones left over before writing the number.

• Point out that students may circle any 10 ones to make 1 ten.

Power Practice
• Have students complete the practice items. Discuss their answers.

WHAT IF THE STUDENT CAN'T

Complete the Power Practice
• Discuss each incorrect answer. Look for common errors such as reversed place value or incorrect counting.

• Have the student show each number with tens and ones models.

Lesson Goal
- Identify and complete a number pattern.

What the Student Needs to Know
- Count by 1s.
- Count by 10s.

Getting Started
Display a hundred chart. Say:
- *Read the first row aloud. Each number in the row is one more than the one before it. 2 is one more than 1. 3 is one more than 2, and so on. So we can say that the pattern for this row is that each number goes up by one.*
- Now *read the last column aloud. What is the pattern?* (Each number goes up by 10.)

What Can I Do?
Read the question and the response. Then read and discuss the examples. Ask:
- *What is true of the ones digits when the pattern is Add One?* (The ones digits go up by 1.)
- *What is true of the ones digits when the pattern is Add Ten?* (The ones digits remain the same.)

Name_____

Number Patterns

Learn

Read this pattern:

36, 37, 38, 39, 40, __?__

Think: 37 is 1 more than 36.
38 is 1 more than 37.
39 is 1 more than 38. The rule is Add One.

Read the Pattern Aloud

Reading aloud helps you "hear" the pattern.
Try reading these numbers aloud.
What number comes next?

44, 45, 46, 47, 48, __?__
23, 33, 43, 53, 63, __?__

Find the Rule

Read this pattern:

34, 44, 54, 64, 74, __?__

Think: 44 is 10 more than 34.
54 is 10 more than 44.
64 is 10 more than 54. The rule is Add Ten.

© McGraw-Hill School Division

106 Grade 2, Chapter 12, Cluster A

WHAT IF THE STUDENT CAN'T

Count by 1s
- Give the student a number to start with; for example, 16. Have the student count by 1s until you say "Stop." Repeat with another starting number until the student seems comfortable counting by 1s from any starting point.

Name_____

1. 11, 21, 31, 41, 51   Add One   (Add Ten)

2. 68, 69, 70, 71, 72   (Add One)   Add Ten

3. 97, 98, 99, 100, 101   (Add One)   Add Ten

4. 46, 56, 66, 76, 86   Add One   (Add Ten)

5. 19, 29, 39, 49, 59   Add One   (Add Ten)

Power Practice • Write the missing numbers in each counting pattern.

6. 20, 30, _40_, 50, 60, _70_

7. 43, _44_, 45, 46, 47, _48_

8. 15, 25, _35_, _45_, 55, 65

9. 26, 27, _28_, 29, _30_, 31

10. 33, 43, _53_, 63, 73, _83_

11. 48, _49_, 50, 51, 52, _53_

12. 42, 52, _62_, _72_, 82, 92

© McGraw-Hill School Division

Grade 2, Chapter 12, Cluster A   **107**

USING THE LESSON

Try It
Counting aloud may help some students to identify the pattern.

Power Practice
- Post a hundred chart for students to refer to if necessary.
- Remind students to check their work by looking at the ones digits in the number patterns.

WHAT IF THE STUDENT CAN'T

Count by 10s
- Provide a hundred chart and have the student read the numbers in the last column. Cover some of the numbers and have the student recite the numbers again. Continue by having the student read the numbers in the other columns.

Complete the Power Practice
- Have the student identify the rule or pattern for each set of numbers.
- Ask the student to count aloud and fill in each missing number.

Lesson Goal

- Compare numbers to 99.

What the Student Needs to Know

- Identify and use the greater than and less than signs.
- Read a number line.
- Read a place-value chart.

Getting Started

Cut out a large tagboard > sign. On the chalkboard, write number pairs such as the following:

- 25   24
- 36   37
- 92   91

Have volunteers come to the board and arrange the symbol so that it points to the lesser number in the pair. Help students read the resulting inequality aloud; for example, "25 is greater than 24." Remind them to read the inequality from left to right, just as they would read any number sentence.

What Can I Do?

Read the question and the response. Then read and discuss the examples. Ask:

- *Does the greater than and less than symbol point to the greater or lesser number?* (lesser)
- *If number Y is to the right of number X on the number line, which number is less?* (number X)
- *If number A has 3 tens, and number B also has 3 tens, how can you tell which number is greater or less?* (Look at the ones place.)

Name_____

Compare Numbers

Learn

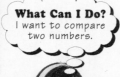

What Can I Do?
I want to compare two numbers.

Use a Number Line

These numbers go up by ones.
Numbers on the right are greater.
Numbers on the left are less.

0 1 2 3 4 5 6 7 8 9 10 11 12 13 14 15 16 17 18 19 20

19 is greater than 9. So 19 > 9.
9 is less than 19. So 9 < 19.

Look at Place Value

Compare the digits in the tens place.
Which digit is greater?

If both digits are the same,
compare the digits in the ones place.
Which digit is greater?

tens	ones
3	5
3	4

Think: 5 ones is greater than 4 ones.
So, 35 is greater than 34.

108 Grade 2, Chapter 12, Cluster B

WHAT IF THE STUDENT CAN'T

Identify and Use the Greater Than and Less Than Signs

- Use your cardboard greater than sign from Getting Started. Show the student how to flip the sign so that it points either to the left or to the right. Remind the student that the arrow should always point to the lesser number. Have the student write two numbers on the chalkboard, use the sign to show the inequality, and read the inequality aloud. Repeat until the student consistently uses the sign correctly.

Read a Number Line

On the chalkboard, draw a 0–10 number line. Ask:

- *Which numbers are greater than 6?* (7, 8, 9, 10)
- *Which numbers are less than 6?* (0, 1, 2,. . .5)
- *If a number is to the left of 6, is it greater or less than 6?* (less)
- *If a number is to the right of 6, is it greater or less than 6?* (greater)

Name_____

Try It . Use the place-value charts.
Circle the number that is greater.

1.
tens	ones
2	5
(5	2)

2.
tens	ones
3	1
(3	2)

3.
tens	ones
(7	3)
5	3

4.
tens	ones
8	7
(8	8)

Power Practice • Compare. Write >, <, or =.

5. 38 (<) 83

6. 44 (>) 43

7. 19 (<) 91

8. 89 (<) 90

9. 27 (>) 25

10. 31 (>) 30

11. 11 (=) 11

12. 65 (>) 55

13. 69 (<) 70

14. 97 (=) 97

15. 78 (<) 79

16. 65 (>) 56

17. 53 (>) 33

18. 30 (>) 3

19. 66 (<) 68

20. 100 (>) 10

© McGraw-Hill School Division

WHAT IF THE STUDENT CAN'T

Read a Place-Value Chart
• Have the student write the numbers in items 5–10 in a place-value chart. Then have the student identify the number of tens and ones in each number and tell which number is greater.

Complete the Power Practice
• Discuss each incorrect answer. If students consistently reverse the symbol, have them read each inequality aloud.
• Students who still have difficulty comparing two-digit numbers should show the numbers using tens and ones models.

Try It
Remind students to look at the tens place first. If those digits are different, they need not look at the ones. If the tens are the same, they must compare the ones.

Power Practice
• Have students complete the practice items. Then review each answer. Discuss the strategies students used to compare the numbers.
• Watch for students who consistently reverse the greater than and "less than" signs. Have these students read their inequalities aloud.

Learn with Partners & Parents
Students can use the ages of members of their households to practice comparing numbers. They should follow these steps:
• List the ages of everyone in your home. If you're not sure, ask.
• Use the ages you found to write as many sentences as possible using the greater than and less than signs. For example, if the ages of people in your home were 8, 10, 38, and 42; you might write:

8 < 10	8 < 38	8 < 42
10 > 8	10 < 38	10 < 42
38 > 8	38 > 10	38 < 42
42 > 8	42 > 10	42 > 38

USING THE LESSON

Lesson Goal
- Order numbers to 99.

What the Student Needs to Know
- Read a hundred chart.
- Count on 1.
- Count back 1.

Getting Started
Give five students number cards 71–75. Have them line up in order in single file and face the class. Ask:
- *Which number comes just after 71? (72) Which number comes just before 74? (73) Which number comes between 73 and 75? (74)*

Continue with similar questions.

What Can I Do?
Read the question and the response. Then read and discuss the examples. Ask:
- *How could you find the number between two numbers on a hundred chart?* (Point to each of the two numbers and name the number in between.)
- *Would you find the number that comes just after a number by counting on or counting back?* (counting on)

Order Numbers

Learn

What Can I Do?
I want to put numbers in order.

Use a Hundred Chart
The numbers are in order from least to greatest.

1	2	3	4	5	6	7	8	9	10
11	12	13	14	15	16	17	18	19	20
21	22	23	24	25	26	27	28	29	30
31	32	33	34	35	36	37	38	39	40
41	42	43	44	45	46	47	48	49	50
51	52	53	54	55	56	57	58	59	60
61	62	63	64	65	66	67	68	69	70
71	72	73	74	75	76	77	78	79	80
81	82	83	84	85	86	87	88	89	90
91	92	93	94	95	96	97	98	99	100

Think: 36 is just before 37.
38 is just after 37.
37 is between 36 and 38.

Count On or Back
Start with one number, such as 78.
Count on 1. One more is 79.
79 is just after 78.

Start with the same number, 78.
Count back 1. One less is 77.
77 is just before 78.
78 is between 77 and 79.

© McGraw-Hill School Division

WHAT IF THE STUDENT CAN'T

Read a Hundred Chart
Display a hundred chart. Ask:
- *What is true of all the numbers in column 5 of the hundred chart?* (They all contain 5 ones.)
- *If you move down the column from row to row, how do the numbers change?* (They increase by 10.)

Count On 1
- Place counters in a line. Have the student count them. Then add one counter and have the student count them again. Repeat with other amounts of counters until the student is comfortable counting on without starting from 1.

Name_____

1. just after 44 __45__

2. between 85 and 87 __86__

3. just before 69 __68__

4. just after 31 __32__

5. between 49 and 51 __50__

6. just before 27 __26__

1	2	3	4	5	6	7	8	9	10
11	12	13	14	15	16	17	18	19	20
21	22	23	24	25	26	27	28	29	30
31	32	33	34	35	36	37	38	39	40
41	42	43	44	45	46	47	48	49	50
51	52	53	54	55	56	57	58	59	60
61	62	63	64	65	66	67	68	69	70
71	72	73	74	75	76	77	78	79	80
81	82	83	84	85	86	87	88	89	90
91	92	93	94	95	96	97	98	99	100

Power Practice . Write the number that comes just before, just after, or between.

7. just after 17 __18__   8. between 55 and 57 __56__

9. just before 96 __95__   10. just after 64 __65__

11. between 76 and 78 __77__   12. just before 21 __20__

13. just after 8 __9__   14. between 93 and 95 __94__

15. just before 2 __1__   16. just after 72 __73__

17. between 81 and 83 __82__   18. just before 100 __99__

19. just after 19 __20__   20. between 19 and 21 __20__

21. just before 40 __39__   22. just after 86 __87__

USING THE LESSON

Try It

- Students should point to the number or numbers on the hundred chart. Then they can move to the right to find the number after, move to the left to find the number before, or move to the middle to find the number between.

- Discuss what happens in item 5, when the numbers given require moving from one row to the next.

Power Practice

- Have the students complete the practice items. Then review each answer. Discuss the strategies students used to order numbers.

WHAT IF THE STUDENT CAN'T

Count Back 1

- Have the student count to 10 and then start at 10 and count back 1. Repeat, having the student count to 6, 13, 21, and 34. Then give the student random numbers between 0 and 99 and have him or her count back 1.

Complete the Power Practice

- Discuss each incorrect answer. Have the student use a hundred chart to correct each answer.

Lesson Goal
- Write as many 3-digit numbers as possible using three given digits.

Introducing the Challenge
Ask the students to name the 2-digit numbers they can make using both of these digits:

- *4 and 5*   (45, 54)
- *1 and 3*   (13, 31)
- *9 and 7*   (97, 79)
- *What 2-digit numbers can you make using the digits 8 and 8? (Only one, 88)*
- *What 2-digit numbers can you make using the digits 6 and 0? (Only one, 60)*

Using the Challenge
- Have students write the answers to the questions before starting to fill in the grids.
- Explain that each digit they write is to be used once in each number. (In other words, if they have the digits 1, 2, and 3; they cannot write 112 as one of their 3-digit numbers.) If any digits are the same, this will limit the number of 3-digit numbers students can make. Not all students will be able to fill all six grids.
- When students have completed the activity, discuss the reasons for their varied answers.

Name_____

Write the Numbers

**Answer the questions.
Then use the digits you write
to write as many different
3-digit numbers as you can.**

How old are you? _____

What is the first digit in your street address? _____

What is the last digit in your phone number? _____

Answers will vary. The number of different 3-digit numbers will range from 1 to 6. If all three digits are different, there will be 6 possible answers. If two digits are the same, there will be 3 possible answers. If one digit is 0 and the other two differ, there should be 4 possible answers. If one digit is 0 and the other two are the same, there should be 2 possible answers. If all three digits are the same, there will be 1 possible answer. Have students compare their answers and discuss the possibilities.

© McGraw-Hill School Division

Changing Patterns

Each of these patterns changes along the way.
Find the rule.
Draw a line where the pattern changes.
The first one is done for you.

1. 2, 4, 6, 8, 10, | 20, 30, 40

2. 5, 10, 15, | 25, 35, 45, 55, 65

3. 10, 20, 30, 40, 50, | 52, 54, 56

4. 2, 12, 22, 32, 42, 52, 62, | 64

5. 8, 18, 28, 38, 48, | 52, 56, 60

6. 100, 90, 80, | 75, 70, 65, 60, 55

7. 41, 43, 45, | 49, 53, 57, 61, 65

8. 35, 135, 235, 335, 435, 535, | 735, 935

CHALLENGE

Lesson Goal
- Identify points where a number pattern changes.

Introducing the Challenge
Have students identify the rule in each of these number patterns.
- *2, 4, 6, 8, 10, 12* (Add Two)
- *3, 6, 9, 12, 15, 18* (Add Three)
- *57, 67, 77, 87, 97* (Add Ten)
- *25, 30, 35, 40, 45* (Add Five)

Using the Challenge
- Read the directions aloud. Have students identify the two rules in item 1. (Add Two, Add Ten)
- Allow students to complete the activity independently. When students have finished, have volunteers share their answers and identify the rules shown in each number pattern. (2. Add Five, Add Ten; 3. Add Ten, Add Two; 4. Add Ten, Add Two; 5. Add Ten, Add Four; 6. Subtract Ten, Subtract Five; 7. Add Two, Add Four; 8. Add 100, Add 200)

Add Tens

Add.

1. 40
+ 10

2. 20
+ 70

3. 50
+ 30

Addition Facts to 20

Add.

4. 8
+ 9

5. 3
+ 7

6. 6
+ 5

Add 2-Digit Numbers

Add.

7. 28
+ 34

8. 32
+ 29

9. 61
+ 15

Round to the Nearest Hundred

**Use the number line. Round each number
to the nearest hundred.**

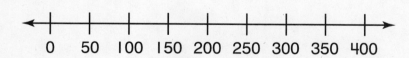

0   50   100   150   200   250   300   350   400

10. 302 _____

11. 185 _____

Subtract Tens

Subtract.

12. 40
   − 10

13. 80
   − 70

14. 60
   − 30

Subtraction Facts to 20

Subtract.

15.   5
   − 2

16. 13
   − 7

17. 16
   − 8

Subtract 2-Digit Numbers

Subtract.

18. 48
   − 23

19. 62
   − 59

20. 31
   − 18

Assessment Goal

This two-page assessment covers skills identified as necessary for success in Chapter 13 Add and Subtract 3-Digit Numbers. The first page assesses the major prerequisite skills for Cluster A. The second page assesses the major prerequisite skills for Cluster B. When the Cluster A and Cluster B prerequisite skills overlap, the skill(s) will be covered in only one section.

Getting Started

- Allow students time to look over the two pages of the assessment. Point out the labels that identify the skills covered.

- Have students find math vocabulary terms used in the assessment. List vocabulary terms on the board as students identify them. If necessary, review the meanings of all essential math vocabulary.

Introducing the Assessment

- Explain to students that these pages will help you know if they are ready to start a new chapter in their math textbooks.

- Students who have transferred from another school may not have been introduced to some of these skills. Encourage students to do their best and assure them you will help them learn any needed skills.

Cluster A Challenge

Those students who demonstrate mastery of the skills on this page will not need to use the reteaching worksheets. Instead, these students can do the Cluster A Challenge found on page 124.

Name _____

Add Tens

Add.

1. 40
  $+10$
  50

2. 20
  $+70$
  90

3. 50
  $+30$
  80

Addition Facts to 20

Add.

4. 8
  $+9$
  17

5. 3
  $+7$
  10

6. 6
  $+5$
  11

Add 2-Digit Numbers

Add.

7. 28
  $+34$
  62

8. 32
  $+29$
  61

9. 61
  $+15$
  76

Round to the Nearest Hundred

Use the number line. Round each number to the nearest hundred.

```
   0  50 100 150 200 250 300 350 400
```

10. 302 ___300___

11. 185 ___200___

© McGraw-Hill School Division

113A Use with Grade 2, Chapter 13, Cluster A

CLUSTER A PREREQUISITE SKILLS

The skills listed in this chart are those identified as major prerequisite skills for students' success in the lessons in Cluster A of the chapter. Each skill is covered by one or more assessment items as shown in the middle column. The right column provides the page numbers for the lessons in this book that reteach the Cluster A prerequisite skills.

Skill Name	Assessment Items	Lesson Pages
Add Tens	1-3	114
Addition Facts to 20	4-6	115
Add 2-Digit Numbers	7-9	116-117
Round to the Nearest Hundred	10-11	118-119

Name _____

Subtract Tens

Subtract.

12. 40
  − 10
  ___
  30

13. 80
  − 70
  ___
  10

14. 60
  − 30
  ___
  30

Subtraction Facts to 20

Subtract.

15. 5
  − 2
  ___
  3

16. 13
  − 7
  ___
  6

17. 16
  − 8
  ___
  8

Subtract 2-Digit Numbers

Subtract.

18. 48
  − 23
  ___
  25

19. 62
  − 59
  ___
  3

20. 31
  − 18
  ___
  13

© McGraw-Hill School Division

Use with Grade 2, Chapter 13, Cluster B **113B**

CLUSTER B PREREQUISITE SKILLS

The skills listed in this chart are those identified as major prerequisite skills for students' success in the lessons in Cluster B of the chapter. Each skill is covered by one or more assessment items as shown in the middle column. The right column provides the page numbers for the lessons in this book that reteach the Cluster B prerequisite skills

Skill Name	Assessment Items	Lesson Pages
Subtract Tens	12-14	120
Subtraction Facts to 20	15-17	121
Subtract 2-Digit Numbers	18-20	122-123

Alternative Assessment Strategies

- Oral administration of the assessment is appropriate for younger students or those whose native language is not English. Read the skills title and directions one section at a time. Check students' understanding by asking them to tell you how they will do the first exercise in the group.
- For some skill types you may wish to use group administration. In this technique, a small group or pair of students complete the assessment together. Through their discussion, you will be able to decide if supplementary reteaching materials are needed.

Intervention Materials

If students are not successful with the prerequisite skills assessed on these pages, reteaching lessons have been created to help them make the transition into the chapter.

Item correlation charts showing the skills lessons suitable for reteaching the prerequisite skills are found beneath the reproductions of each page of the assessment.

Cluster B Challenge
Those students who demonstrate mastery of the skills on this page will not need to use the reteaching worksheets. Instead, these students can do the Cluster B Challenge found on page 125.

Lesson Goal
- Add multiples of ten.

What the Student Needs to Know
- Add facts to 10.
- Use tens models.

Getting Started
- Have students count by 10s to 100.
- Display a hundred chart and have students locate the 10s. (10, 20, 30, . . . 100)

What Can I Do?
Read the question and the response. Then read and discuss the examples. Ask:
- *If 2 + 3 = 5, what is 20 + 30?* (50) *Why?* (2 ones plus 3 ones equals 5 ones, so 2 tens plus 3 tens equals 5 tens.)

Try It
Have students complete the addition sentences in this section. Ask students to read the addition sentences and their answers aloud.

Power Practice
- Have students complete the practice items. Then review each answer.
- Watch for students who leave out the zero in their answers.

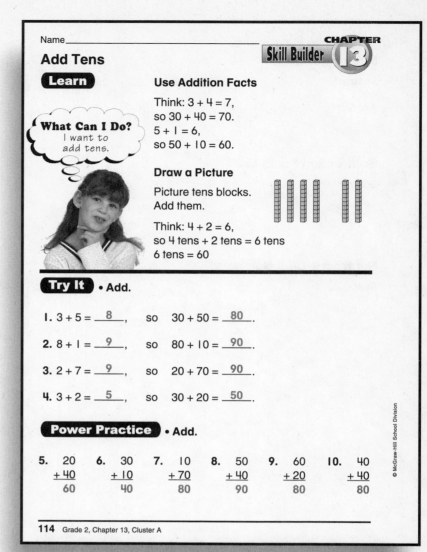

Name _____

Add Tens

Learn

What Can I Do? I want to add tens.

Use Addition Facts

Think: $3 + 4 = 7$,
so $30 + 40 = 70$.
$5 + 1 = 6$,
so $50 + 10 = 60$.

Draw a Picture

Picture tens blocks. Add them.

Think: $4 + 2 = 6$,
so 4 tens + 2 tens = 6 tens
6 tens = 60

Try It · Add.

1. $3 + 5 = \underline{8}$, so $30 + 50 = \underline{80}$.

2. $8 + 1 = \underline{9}$, so $80 + 10 = \underline{90}$.

3. $2 + 7 = \underline{9}$, so $20 + 70 = \underline{90}$.

4. $3 + 2 = \underline{5}$, so $30 + 20 = \underline{50}$.

Power Practice · Add.

5.	6.	7.	8.	9.	10.
20	30	10	50	60	40
+40	+10	+70	+40	+20	+40
60	40	80	90	80	80

© McGraw-Hill School Division

114 Grade 2, Chapter 13, Cluster A

WHAT IF THE STUDENT CAN'T

Add Facts to 10
- Write addition facts on flash cards and have students work in pairs to quiz each other.
- Review facts to 10. Have students write the facts that still cause them difficulty, take them home, and practice them with a parent or sibling.

Use Tens Models
- Give the student a handful of tens models and have him or her count by tens to find the total represented. Take some models away and have the student find the total again. Add some models and repeat.

Complete the Power Practice
- Give the student tens models and have him or her model any incorrect items.
- Remind students to add the ones before adding the tens, just as they would for any 2-digit number. This will prevent their forgetting the placeholder zero.

Name_____

Addition Facts to 20

Learn

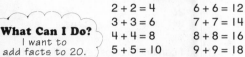

What Can I Do?
I want to add facts to 20.

Use Doubles

Think about doubles.

$2 + 2 = 4$	$6 + 6 = 12$
$3 + 3 = 6$	$7 + 7 = 14$
$4 + 4 = 8$	$8 + 8 = 16$
$5 + 5 = 10$	$9 + 9 = 18$

Think: $5 + 6$ is like $5 + 5 + 1$.
$5 + 6 = 11$

$8 + 7$ is like $8 + 8 - 1$.
$8 + 7 = 15$

Use Turnaround Facts

If you know one fact, then you really know two facts.

Think: $4 + 5 = 9$, so $5 + 4 = 9$.
$8 + 6 = 14$, so $6 + 8 = 14$.

	tens	ones
		6
+		7
	1	3

Try It • Add.

1. $5 + 5 = \underline{10}$, so $5 + 4 = \underline{9}$.

2. $7 + 7 = \underline{14}$, so $7 + 6 = \underline{13}$.

3. $9 + 9 = \underline{18}$, so $9 + 10 = \underline{19}$.

4. $7 + 4 = \underline{11}$, so $4 + 7 = \underline{11}$.

Power Practice • Add

5. 7	6. 2	7. 9	8. 6	9. 3	10. 9
+8	+9	+4	+8	+7	+6
15	11	13	14	10	15

© McGraw-Hill School Division

Grade 2, Chapter 13, Cluster A **115**

WHAT IF THE STUDENT CAN'T

Add Doubles

- Make flash cards with doubles from $1 + 1$ to $6 + 6$. Have students work in pairs to practice adding doubles.

Add or Subtract One

- Mix number cards 1–9 and place them face down. Have the student turn up a card, add 1, and give the sum. Repeat until all cards have been turned up. Then mix the cards and repeat the game, having the student subtract 1 this time.

Use the Commutative Property of Addition

- On index cards, write numbers from fact families such as 3, 4, 7; 2, 8, 10; 7, 6, 13; 4, 8, 12; and so on. Have the student pick a card and write the two addition sentences that can be made with those numbers. Repeat with other cards.

Complete the Power Practice

- Discuss each incorrect answer. Have the student model any fact he or she missed using counters.

USING THE LESSON

Lesson Goal
- Add facts to 20.

What the Student Needs to Know
- Add doubles.
- Add or subtract one.
- Use the Commutative Property of Addition.

Getting Started
- Hold up flash cards with facts to 20 and have students take turns giving the sums. Ask students to write any facts that still cause them trouble. They should practice these facts at home.

What Can I Do?
Read the question and the response. Then read and discuss the examples. Ask:
- *How does knowing 5 + 5 help you know 5 + 6?* (Because 6 is 1 more than 5, the answer will be 1 more than 10, or 11.)
- *How does knowing 8 + 8 help you know 8 + 7?* (Because 7 is 1 less than 8, the answer will be 1 less than 16, or 15.)

Try It
You may wish to have students describe the relationship between the sentences in each pair before finding the sums.

Power Practice
- Ask students to skim the items and answer the ones that are easiest for them first before going back to the others.
- Have students complete the practice items. Then review each answer.

Lesson Goal
• Add 2-digit numbers, with and without regrouping.

What the Student Needs to Know
• Regroup ones as tens and ones.
• Check addition.

Getting Started
Use tens and ones models to show the numbers 13 and 18. Ask:

• *How many tens are in each number? How many ones are in each number?* (1 ten, 3 ones; 1 ten, 8 ones)

Put the models together. Say:

• *I'm adding 13 and 18. Now how many tens do I have? How many ones do I have?* (2 tens, 11 ones)

• *What can I do with 11 ones?* (Regroup as 1 ten and 1 one.)

• *Now how many tens do I have? How many ones do I have?* (3 tens, 1 one)

What Can I Do?
Read the question and the response. Then read and discuss the examples. Ask:

• *Why can you add 6 ones and 3 ones without regrouping?* (They add up to 9 ones, which is less than the 10 ones needed for regrouping.)

• *Why do you need to regroup when you add 6 ones and 7 ones?* (They add up to 13 ones, which is more than 10 ones or 1 ten.)

Add 2-Digit Numbers

Learn

Decide Whether to Regroup

$$\begin{array}{r} 26 \\ + 43 \\ \hline \end{array} \qquad \begin{array}{r} 26 \\ + 47 \\ \hline \end{array}$$

Think: I can add 6 ones and 3 ones without regrouping. I can't add 6 ones and 7 ones without regrouping.

No Regrouping   Regroup 13 ones as 1 ten 3 ones.

What Can I Do?
I want to add 2-digit numbers.

$$\begin{array}{r} 26 \\ + 43 \\ \hline 69 \end{array} \qquad \begin{array}{r} {}^{1} \\ 26 \\ + 47 \\ \hline 73 \end{array}$$

Add the Other Way to Check

Check addition by adding in the other direction.

$$\begin{array}{r} 43 \\ + 26 \\ \hline 69 \end{array} \qquad \begin{array}{r} {}^{1} \\ 47 \\ + 26 \\ \hline 73 \end{array}$$

Try It • Circle *Regroup* or *No Regrouping*. Then add.

1. $\begin{array}{r} 55 \\ + 34 \\ \hline 89 \end{array}$ Regroup   (No Regrouping)

WHAT IF THE STUDENT CAN'T

Regroup Ones as Tens and Ones
• Give the student 18 ones models and 5 tens models. Have the student show addends like these: 32 + 18; 17 + 25; 29 + 17. After showing the addends, have the student put the models together and regroup any groups of 10 ones for 1 ten before finding the sum. Encourage the student to talk about each step of the process.

Check Addition
• Display addition fact cards to 18 and have the student use counters to model the facts.

• Then ask the student to check the addition by adding the numbers in a different direction and using counters to model the new fact.

2. 28 (Regroup) No Regrouping
    + 17
    45

3. 24 (Regroup) No Regrouping
    + 48
    72

Power Practice • Add. Check by adding in the other direction.

4. 32
    + 8
    40

5. 40
    + 22
    62

6. 57
    + 27
    84

7. 33
    + 29
    62

8. 64
    + 31
    95

9. 65
    + 6
    71

10. 42
    + 52
    94

11. 35
    + 45
    80

12. 86
    + 12
    98

13. 14
    + 68
    82

14. 21
    + 67
    88

15. 47
    + 39
    86

16. 13
    + 18
    31

17. 53
    + 8
    61

18. 46
    + 19
    65

USING THE LESSON

Try It
• Remind students that they need only look at the ones digits to know whether or not to regroup. If the ones add up to less than 10, no regrouping is needed. If they add up to 10 or more, you must regroup.
• Make sure students realize that they are to add as well as to circle the correct choice.

Power Practice
• If necessary, provide additional paper for students to check their answers.
• Have students complete the practice items. Then review each answer.

WHAT IF THE STUDENT CAN'T

Complete the Power Practice
• Discuss each incorrect answer. Have the student tell which addition problems require regrouping and which do not.

• Watch for students who consistently fail to add the regrouped ten. Remind them to write the 1 above the tens after they add the ones.

Lesson Goal
- Round numbers to the nearest hundred.

What the Student Needs to Know
- Read a number line.
- Identify the tens digit.

Getting Started
Have students count by 100s to 1,000. Say:

- *222 is between 200 and 300. Between which two hundreds is 450? 760? 546? 812?* (400 and 500; 700 and 800; 500 and 600; 800 and 900)

What Can I Do?
Read the question and the response. Then read and discuss the examples. Ask:

- *What does it mean when you say "222 rounds down to 200"?* (200 is the nearest hundred to 222, and it is less, so you have to round down.)
- *What does it mean when you say "275 rounds up to 300"?* (300 is the nearest hundred to 275, and it is greater, so you have to round up.)
- *Would you round 450 up or down? Why?* (Up; you round up when the tens digit is 5 or greater.)

Try It
Suggest that students use these steps:

- Find the number on the number line.
- Find the hundreds on either side of that number.
- Decide which hundred is closer to the number.
- Write that hundred.

Name_____

Learn

Use a Number Line

The number 222 is between 200 and 300. It is closer to 200.

So 222 rounds down to 200.

The number 275 is between 200 and 300. It is closer to 300.

So 275 rounds up to 300.

What Can I Do? I want to round a number to the nearest hundred.

```
        222  275
         ▼    ▼
|--+--+--+--⊕+⊕--+-->
0  50 100 150 200 250 300
```

Use the Digit in the Tens Place

Look at the tens digit.
If it is less than 5, round down.
If it is 5 or greater, round up.

Round 149 down to 100.
Round 150 up to 200.

Try It • Use the number line.
Round to the nearest hundred.

1. 130 __100__
```
<--+--+--+--+--+--+--+--+--+--+-->
 100 110 120 130 140 150 160 170 180 190 200
```

2. 580 __600__
```
<--+--+--+--+--+--+--+--+--+--+-->
 500 510 520 530 540 550 560 570 580 590 600
```

3. 320 __300__
```
<--+--+--+--+--+--+--+--+--+--+-->
 300 310 320 330 340 350 360 370 380 390 400
```

118 Grade 2, Chapter 13, Cluster A

WHAT IF THE STUDENT CAN'T

Read a Number Line
- On the board, draw a number line that is marked in 10s from 100 to 200. Cover up or erase some of the numbers and have the student fill them in.
- Use the number line above. Have the student locate (1) two numbers that are greater than 110; (2) two numbers that are less than 150. Continue with other numbers.

Identify the Tens Digit
- Have students use items 1–5 in Try It. Ask them to write the five numbers and underline the tens digits.

Name_____

4. 258 _300_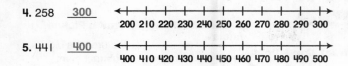
200 210 220 230 240 250 260 270 280 290 300

5. 441 _400_
400 410 420 430 440 450 460 470 480 490 500

Power Practice • Round each number to the nearest hundred.

6. 730 _700_   **7.** 195 _200_

8. 253 _300_   **9.** 543 _500_

10. 236 _200_   **11.** 858 _900_

12. 142 _100_   **13.** 659 _700_

14. 75 _100_   **15.** 360 _400_

16. 715 _700_   **17.** 907 _900_

18. 455 _500_   **19.** 346 _300_

20. 188 _200_   **21.** 220 _200_

USING THE LESSON

Power Practice

- If students have trouble, they might draw a number line to help them.

- Have students complete the practice items. Then review each answer.

Learn with Partners & Parents

Have students use books in their classroom or at home to practice rounding.

- Choose ten books. Each book should have at least 50 pages. Look at the page number on the last page of each one.

- Round the number of pages to the nearest hundred.

- How many books have page numbers that round to 100? That round to 200 or 300? Write their titles.

WHAT IF THE STUDENT CAN'T

Complete the Power Practice

- Discuss each incorrect answer. Review the rules for rounding: down if the tens digit is 0–4, up if the tens digit is 5–9 to the nearest hundred.

- Have students circle the tens digit before rounding the number.

Lesson Goal
• Subtract multiples of ten.

What the Student Needs to Know
• Subtract facts to 10.
• Use tens models.

Getting Started
• Have students count by 10s to 100. Then have them count backward by 10s from 100 to 0.

What Can I Do?
Read the question and the response. Then read and discuss the examples. Ask:
• *If 8 – 3 = 5, what is 80 – 30?* (50) *Why?* (8 ones minus 3 ones equals 5 ones; 8 tens minus 3 tens equals 5 tens)

Try It
Have students complete the subtraction sentence in this section. Then ask them to read the sentences and their answers aloud.

Power Practice
• Have students complete the practice items. Then review each answer.
• Watch for students who leave out the zero in the final answer.

Name_____

Subtract Tens

Learn

What Can I Do? I want to subtract tens.

Use Subtraction Facts

Think: 9 – 4 = 5, so 90 – 40 = 50.

6 – 3 = 3, so 60 – 30 = 30.

Draw a Picture

Picture tens blocks. Subtract them.

Think: 5 – 2 = 3, so 5 tens – 2 tens = 3 tens.
3 tens = 30

Try It • Subtract.

1. 6 – 5 = __1__, so 60 – 50 = __10__.

2. 7 – 2 = __5__, so 70 – 20 = __50__.

3. 4 – 1 = __3__, so 40 – 10 = __30__.

4. 8 – 4 = __4__, so 80 – 40 = __40__.

Power Practice • Subtract.

5. 40	6. 30	7. 60	8. 50	9. 70	10. 90
− 30	− 10	− 40	− 30	− 40	− 50
10	20	20	20	30	40

© McGraw-Hill School Division

120 Grade 2, Chapter 13, Cluster B

WHAT IF THE STUDENT CAN'T

Subtract Facts to 10
• Write subtraction facts on flash cards and have students work in pairs to quiz each other.
• Review facts to 10. Have students write the facts that still cause them difficulty, take them home, and practice them with a parent or sibling.

Use Tens Models
• Give the student a handful of tens models and have him or her count by tens to find the total represented. Take some models away and have the student find the total again. Add some models and repeat.

• Ask the student to use tens models to show the following numbers: 30, 50, 90, 10, 60.

Complete the Power Practice
• Give the student tens models and have him or her use them to model any incorrect items.
• Remind the student to subtract the ones before subtracting the tens, as in any 2-digit substraction. This will prevent their forgetting the placeholder zero.

Subtraction Facts to 20

Learn

Use Doubles

Think about doubles.

2 + 2 = 4	4 − 2 = 2
3 + 3 = 6	6 − 3 = 3
4 + 4 = 8	8 − 4 = 4
5 + 5 = 10	10 − 5 = 5
6 + 6 = 12	12 − 6 = 6
7 + 7 = 14	14 − 7 = 7
8 + 8 = 16	16 − 8 = 8
9 + 9 = 18	18 − 9 = 9

Think: 13 − 6 is one more than 12 − 6.

13 − 6 = 7

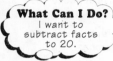

What Can I Do?
I want to subtract facts to 20.

Use Fact Families

If you know one fact, then you may know other facts.

	tens	ones
	1	6
−		9
		7

Think: 15 − 8 = 7, so 15 − 7 = 8.
9 − 3 = 6, so 9 − 6 = 3.

Try It • Subtract.

1. 14 − 7 = __7__, so 15 − 7 = __8__.

2. 10 − 5 = __5__, so 11 − 5 = __6__.

3. 6 − 3 = __3__, so 7 − 3 = __4__.

Power Practice • Subtract.

4. 11 − 8 = __3__   5. 14 − 9 = __5__   6. 17 − 8 = __9__

WHAT IF THE STUDENT CAN'T

Add Doubles
- Work with the student, using doubles flash cards each from 1 + 1 to 9 + 9. Continue for 10 minutes each day until the students can say each each answer without hesitation.

Recognize the Relationship Between Addition and Subtraction
- For each flash card from the above activity, have the student write the related subtraction fact.

Identify Fact Families
- Challenge the student to write all four facts in the family for the following numbers: 4, 6, 10; 8, 6, 14; 9, 8, 17; 6, 5, 11.

Complete the Power Practice
- Discuss each incorrect answer. Have the student model any fact he or she missed using counters.

USING THE LESSON

Lesson Goal
- Subtract facts to 20.

What the Student Needs to Know
- Add doubles.
- Recognize the relationship between addition and subtraction.
- Identify fact families.

Getting Started
Give each group of students 18 counters. Have them model these subtraction facts as you read them aloud.
- 14 − 8
- 10 − 6
- 17 − 9
- 13 − 4

What Can I Do?
Read the question and the response. Then read and discuss the examples. Ask:
- *How does knowing 2 + 2 = 4 help you know 4 − 2 = 2?* (because subtraction is the opposite of addition)
- *How does knowing 5 − 3 = 2 help you know 5 − 2 = 3?* (because the numbers are part of a fact family)

Try It
You may wish to have students describe the relationship between the sentences in each pair before finding the differences.

Power Practice
- Have students complete the practice items. Then review each answer.

Lesson Goal
- Subtract 2-digit numbers, with and without regrouping.

What the Student Needs to Know
- Regroup tens and ones as ones.
- Check subtraction.

Getting Started
Use tens and ones models to show the number 43. Ask:

- *How many tens are there? How many ones are there?* (4 tens, 3 ones)

Say:

- *I want to subtract 15. How many tens and ones is that?* (1 ten, 5 ones)

- *How can I subtract 5 ones when I only have 3 ones?* (Regroup 1 ten as 10 ones, add it to the 3 ones to make 13 ones.)

- *Now how many tens do I have? How many ones do I have?* (3 tens, 13 ones) *So if I subtract 5 ones, I have 8 ones left. If I subtract 1 ten, I have 2 tens left. My answer is 2 tens, 8 ones, or 28.*

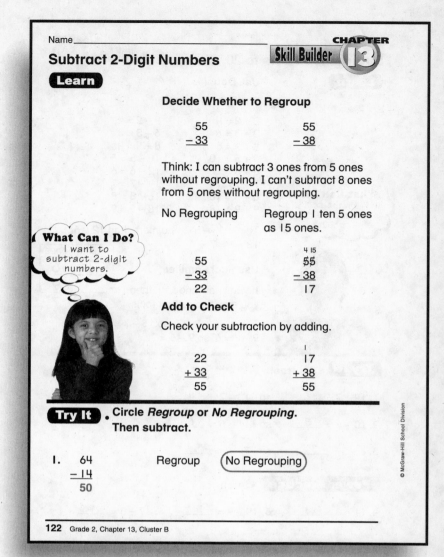

Name_____

Subtract 2-Digit Numbers

Skill Builder

CHAPTER 13

Learn

Decide Whether to Regroup

$$\begin{array}{r} 55 \\ -33 \end{array} \qquad \begin{array}{r} 55 \\ -38 \end{array}$$

Think: I can subtract 3 ones from 5 ones without regrouping. I can't subtract 8 ones from 5 ones without regrouping.

No Regrouping   Regroup 1 ten 5 ones as 15 ones.

$$\begin{array}{r} 55 \\ -33 \\ \hline 22 \end{array} \qquad \begin{array}{r} {}^{4}\;{}^{15} \\ 5\!\!\!5 \\ -38 \\ \hline 17 \end{array}$$

What Can I Do?
I want to subtract 2-digit numbers.

Add to Check

Check your subtraction by adding.

$$\begin{array}{r} 22 \\ +33 \\ \hline 55 \end{array} \qquad \begin{array}{r} {}^{1} \\ 17 \\ +38 \\ \hline 55 \end{array}$$

Try It . Circle *Regroup* or *No Regrouping*. Then subtract.

1. $\begin{array}{r} 64 \\ -14 \\ \hline 50 \end{array}$ Regroup   (No Regrouping)

© McGraw-Hill School Division

122 Grade 2, Chapter 13, Cluster B

WHAT IF THE STUDENT CAN'T

Regroup Tens and Ones as Ones
- Give the student 5 tens models and 15 ones models. Have the student show numbers like these: 43, 25, 32. After modeling the numbers, have the student demonstrate how to subtract 15 from each number, regrouping 1 ten as 10 ones where needed. Encourage the student to talk about each step in the process.

Check Addition
- Display subtraction fact cards to 18 and have the student tell the difference and explain how he or she might add to check.

- Ask the student to write the addition fact for each subtraction fact.

2. 50
    − 25
    ‾‾‾‾
     25
    (Regroup)   No Regrouping

3. 83
    − 14
    ‾‾‾‾
     69
    (Regroup)   No Regrouping

Power Practice • Subtract. Check by adding.

4. 92   **5.** 45   **6.** 56
    − 6   − 32   − 17
    ‾‾‾‾   ‾‾‾‾   ‾‾‾‾
     86   13   39

7. 82   **8.** 56   **9.** 98
    − 48   − 21   − 57
    ‾‾‾‾   ‾‾‾‾   ‾‾‾‾
     34   35   41

10. 72   **11.** 85   **12.** 36
     − 58   − 29   − 18
     ‾‾‾‾   ‾‾‾‾   ‾‾‾‾
      14   56   18

13. 66   **14.** 74   **15.** 48
     − 65   − 26   − 29
     ‾‾‾‾   ‾‾‾‾   ‾‾‾‾
       1   48   19

16. 63   **17.** 47   **18.** 59
     − 35   − 28   − 21
     ‾‾‾‾   ‾‾‾‾   ‾‾‾‾
      28   19   38

USING THE LESSON

What Can I Do?

Read the question and the response. Then read and discuss the examples. Ask:

- *Why can you subtract 3 ones from 5 ones without regrouping?* (3 is less than 5.)
- *Why do you need to regroup when you subtract 8 ones from 5 ones?* (8 is greater than 5, and you can't subtract a greater number from a lesser number.)

Try It

- Remind students that they need only look at the ones digits to know whether or not to regroup. If there are more ones in the number being subtracted, you must regroup.
- Make sure students complete each subtraction, as well as circling the correct choice.

Power Practice

- Provide additional paper, if necessary, so that students can check their answers.
- Have students complete the practice items. Then review each answer.

WHAT IF THE STUDENT CAN'T

Complete the Power Practice

- Discuss each incorrect answer. Have the student tell which subtraction problems require regrouping and which do not.

- Watch for students who consistently have answers that are too great by ten. Remind them to cross out the tens and write 1 less ten whenever regrouping occurs.

CHALLENGE

Lesson Goal
• Find the missing digits in 3-digit addition problems.

Introducing the Challenge
• Write the following addition problems on the board and have students find the missing digits.

$$6\square^{(6)} \qquad \square 3^{(3)}$$
$$\underline{+21} \qquad \underline{+46}$$
$$87 \qquad 7\square^{(9)}$$

Ask students to explain the strategies they used to find the missing digits.

Using the Challenge
• Read the directions aloud. Provide place-value models for those students who need them.
• When students have solved the problems, discuss how knowing addition facts, turn-around facts, and the fact that subtraction is the opposite of addition helped them.

Missing Numbers
Use place-value models if you need them.
Write the missing numbers.

1.

hundreds	tens	ones
3	**6**	5
+ 3	4	6
7	1	**1**

2.

hundreds	tens	ones
1	2	5
+ 3	**8**	5
5	1	**0**

3.

hundreds	tens	ones
6	**6**	2
+ 2	4	3
9	0	**5**

4.

hundreds	tens	ones
2	**3**	5
+ **3**	6	7
6	0	**2**

5.

hundreds	tens	ones
1	**7**	9
+ **1**	4	5
3	2	**4**

6.

hundreds	tens	ones
1	9	7
+ 5	**4**	4
7	4	**1**

7.

hundreds	tens	ones
2	**8**	8
+ 4	5	**5**
7	4	3

8.

hundreds	tens	ones
3	**8**	8
+ **5**	4	5
9	3	**3**

Name_____

CHALLENGE **13**

Missing Number Train

Use place-value models if you need them.
Write the missing numbers.

Hint: An arrow always points to the same number that it came from.

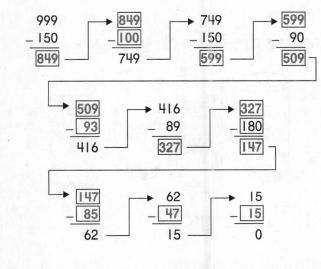

$$999 - 150 = \boxed{849}$$
$$\boxed{849} - \boxed{100} = 749$$
$$749 - 150 = \boxed{599}$$
$$\boxed{599} - 90 = \boxed{509}$$

$$\boxed{509} - \boxed{93} = 416$$
$$416 - 89 = \boxed{327}$$
$$\boxed{327} - \boxed{180} = \boxed{147}$$

$$\boxed{147} - \boxed{85} = 62$$
$$62 - \boxed{47} = 15$$
$$15 - \boxed{15} = 0$$

Grade 2, Chapter 13, Cluster B **125**

CHALLENGE

Lesson Goal
• Subtract 2- and 3-digit numbers in a number line.

Introducing the Challenge
• Give each student 12 counters. Say:
• *Subtract 2. Say the number sentence.* (12 – 2 = 10)
• *Now subtract 3. Say the number sentence.* (10 – 3 = 7)
• *Now subtract 5. Say the number sentence.* (7 – 5 = 2)
• *Now subtract 2. Say the number sentence.* (2 – 2 = 0)

Using the Challenge
• Read the directions aloud. You may want to do the first two problems with students.
• Then have students complete the activity independently. Provide place-value models for those who need them.
• Discuss students' answers and ask students to explain how they figured out the missing numbers.

Skip Counting

Write the missing numbers.

1. 2, 4, 6, _____, 10, 12, _____

2. 3, 6, _____, 12, 15, _____, 21

Equal Groups

Write how many groups. Write how many are in each group.

3.

_____ groups of _____

4.

_____ groups of _____

Write a Number Sentence

Write a number sentence for each picture.

5.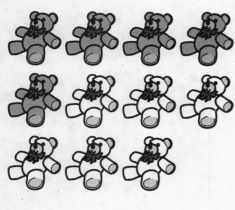

_____ + _____ = _____

6.

_____ ◯ _____ ◯ _____

Equal Groups

Draw lines to show the number of equal groups.

7. Make 3 equal groups.

8. Make 5 equal groups.

9. Make 4 equal groups.

10. Make 2 equal groups.

CHAPTER 14 PRE-CHAPTER ASSESSMENT

Assessment Goal

This two-page assessment covers skills identified as necessary for success in Chapter 14 Multiplication and Division. The first page assesses the major prerequisite skills for Cluster A. The second page assesses the major prerequisite skills for Cluster B. When the Cluster A and Cluster B prerequisite skills overlap, the skill(s) will be covered in only one section.

Getting Started

- Allow students time to look over the two pages of the assessment. Point out the labels that identify the skills covered.
- Have students find math vocabulary terms used in the assessment. List vocabulary terms on the board as students identify them. If necessary, review the meanings of all essential math vocabulary.

Introducing the Assessment

- Explain to students that these pages will help you know if they are ready to start a new chapter in their math textbooks.
- Students who have transferred from another school may not have been introduced to some of these skills. Encourage students to do their best and assure them you will help them learn any needed skills.

Cluster A Challenge

Those students who demonstrate mastery of the skills on this page will not need to use the reteaching worksheets. Instead, these students can do the Cluster A Challenge found on page 134.

Name _____

Skip Counting

Write the missing numbers.

1. 2, 4, 6, ___8___, 10, 12, ___14___

2. 3, 6, ___9___, 12, 15, ___18___, 21

Equal Groups

Write how many groups. Write how many are in each group.

3.

___3___ groups of ___6___

4.

___4___ groups of ___2___

Write a Number Sentence

Write a number sentence for each picture.

5.

___5___ + ___6___ = ___11___

6.

___14___ ⊝ ___5___ ⊜ ___9___

© McGraw-Hill School Division

125A Use with Grade 2, Chapter 14, Cluster A

CLUSTER A PREREQUISITE SKILLS

The skills listed in this chart are those identified as major prerequisite skills for students' success in the lessons in Cluster A of the chapter. Each skill is covered by one or more assessment items as shown in the middle column. The right column provides the page numbers for the lessons in this book that reteach the Cluster A prerequisite skills.

Skill Name	Assessment Items	Lesson Pages
Skip Counting	1-2	126-127
Equal Groups	3-4	128-129
Write a Number Sentence	5-6	130-131

Equal Groups

Draw lines to show the number of equal groups.

7. Make 3 equal groups.

8. Make 5 equal groups.

9. Make 4 equal groups.

10. Make 2 equal groups.

CLUSTER B PREREQUISITE SKILLS

The skills listed in this chart are those identified as major prerequisite skills for students' success in the lessons in Cluster B of the chapter. Each skill is covered by one or more assessment items as shown in the middle column. The right column provides the page numbers for the lessons in this book that reteach the Cluster B prerequisite skills

Skill Name	Assessment Items	Lesson Pages
Equal Groups	7-10	132-133

Alternative Assessment Strategies

- Oral administration of the assessment is appropriate for younger students or those whose native language is not English. Read the skills title and directions one section at a time. Check students' understanding by asking them to tell you how they will do the first exercise in the group.

- For some skill types you may wish to use group administration. In this technique, a small group or pair of students complete the assessment together. Through their discussion, you will be able to decide if supplementary reteaching materials are needed.

Intervention Materials

If students are not successful with the prerequisite skills assessed on these pages, reteaching lessons have been created to help them make the transition into the chapter.

Item correlation charts showing the skills lessons suitable for reteaching the prerequisite skills are found beneath the reproductions of each page of the assessment.

Cluster B Challenge

Those students who demonstrate mastery of the skills on this page will not need to use the reteaching worksheets. Instead, these students can do the Cluster B Challenge found on page 135.

Lesson Goal

• Skip count by 2s, 3s, 4s, or 5s.

What the Student Needs to Know

• Read a hundred chart.

• Complete a number pattern.

Getting Started

Line up twelve students. Have them count off by 1s. Give each student a number card from 1–12 to hold up. Then ask every other student to step forward. Ask:

• *What numbers do you see?* (2, 4, 6, 8, 10, 12) *That's the same as counting by 2s.*

Realign the students and ask every third student to step forward. Ask:

• *What numbers do you see now?* (3, 6, 9, 12) *That's the same as counting by 3s.*

Repeat, asking every fourth student to step forward. (4, 8, 12)

What Can I Do?

Read the question and the response. Then read and discuss the examples. Ask:

• *What is true about all the numbers you count when you count by 5s?* (The ones digit is either 5 or 0.)

• *When you count by 2s and by 4s, the numbers you count have some things in common. What are they?* (They are even numbers; the numbers you count when you count by 4s are also numbers you count when you count by 2s.)

Name_____

Skip Counting

Learn

Use a Hundred Chart

A hundred chart shows all the numbers from 1 to 100.

1	2	3	4	5	6	7	8	9	10
11	12	13	14	15	16	17	18	19	20
21	22	23	24	25	26	27	28	29	30
31	32	33	34	35	36	37	38	39	40
41	42	43	44	45	46	47	48	49	50
51	52	53	54	55	56	57	58	59	60
61	62	63	64	65	66	67	68	69	70
71	72	73	74	75	76	77	78	79	80
81	82	83	84	85	86	87	88	89	90
91	92	93	94	95	96	97	98	99	100

Start at 2. Stop at every other number.
Start at 3. Stop at every 3rd number.
Start at 4. Stop at every 4th number.
Start at 5. Stop at every 5th number.

Use Number Patterns

What Can I Do?
I want to skip count by 2s, 3s, 4s, or 5s.

Look at the ones digits when you count
by 2s: 2 4 6 8 10 12 14 16 18 20
by 4s: 4 8 12 16 20 24 28 32 36 40
by 5s: 5 10 15 20 25 30 35 40 45 50

Count by 3s. The digits in each number should add up to 3, 6, or 9.

3 6 9 12 15 18 21 24 27

For greater numbers, add the digits. Then add again.

75   7 + 5 = 12   1 + 2 = 3

© McGraw-Hill School Division

WHAT IF THE STUDENT CAN'T

Read a Hundred Chart

• Display a hundred chart. Have the student identify all the numbers that have 5 in the ones place (5, 15, 25,. . . 95) and all the numbers that have 0 in the ones place (10, 20, 30,. . .100). Then have the student point to each number as he or she counts by 2s.

Complete a Number Pattern

Have the student continue each of these patterns by saying the next three numbers:

• 15, 20, 25, 30, ?, ?, ? (35, 40, 45)

• 42, 44, 46, 48, ?, ?, ? (50, 52, 54)

• 63, 66, 69, 72, ?, ?, ? (75, 78, 81)

• 12, 16, 20, 24, ?, ?, ? (28, 32, 36)

Name_____

Try It • Fill in the missing numbers.

1.

1	2	3	4	5	6	7	8	9	10
11	12	13	14	15	16	17	18	19	20
21	22	23	24	25	26	27	28	29	30
31	32	33	34	35	36	37	38	39	40

2.

71	72	73	74	75	76	77	78	79	80
81	82	83	84	85	86	87	88	89	90
91	92	93	94	95	96	97	98	99	100

Power Practice • Write the missing numbers in each skip counting pattern.

3. 60, __65__, 70, 75, 80, __85__

4. 21, 24, __27__, __30__, 33, 36

5. 64, 68, __72__, 76, __80__, 84

6. 40, 44, __48__, 52, __56__, 60

7. 30, 35, __40__, __45__, 50, 55

8. 86, 88, __90__, __92__, __94__, 96

9. 54, 57, __60__, __63__, 66, 69

10. 62, __64__, 66, 68, 70, __72__

© McGraw-Hill School Division

Grade 2, Chapter 14, Cluster A **127**

USING THE LESSON

Try It

Some students may need to count aloud to fill in the missing numbers.

Power Practice

• Tell students to figure out the rule before filling in the missing numbers.

• Have students complete the practice items. Tell them to look back at the hundred chart if they have trouble.

WHAT IF THE STUDENT CAN'T

Complete the Power Practice

• Ask the student to identify the rule for each pattern. For example, for item 3 the rule might be "Add Five" or "Count by 5s."

• Refer the student back to the number pattern rules shown on page 126. Have him or her apply those rules to any incorrect items.

Grade 2, Chapter 14, Cluster A **127**

Lesson Goal

- Identify equal groups and the number within each group.

What the Student Needs to Know

- Count groups.
- Recognize the meaning of "equal groups."

Getting Started

Give each pair of students 12 counters. Say:

- *Make a group of 6. How many are left? (6) Do you have equal groups? (yes) How many equal groups do you have? (2)*
- *Now make groups of 4. How many equal groups do you have? (3)*
- *Make groups of 3. How many equal groups do you have? (4)*
- *Make 2 groups that are not equal. (Answers will vary.)*

What Can I Do?

Read the question and the response. Then read and discuss the examples. Ask:

- *What is the difference between equal groups and groups that are not equal?* (Equal groups have the same number of items. Groups that are not equal have different numbers of items.)
- Draw 8 circles. Ask a volunteer to draw equal groups of objects in each circle. Discuss different ways of doing this.

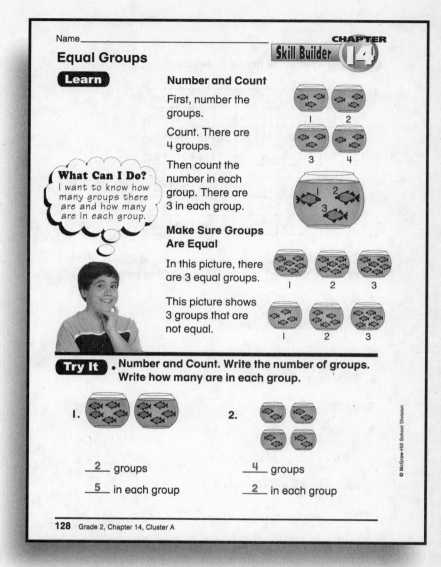

Name_____

Equal Groups

Learn

Number and Count

First, number the groups.

Count. There are 4 groups.

Then count the number in each group. There are 3 in each group.

What Can I Do? I want to know how many groups there are and how many are in each group.

Make Sure Groups Are Equal

In this picture, there are 3 equal groups.

This picture shows 3 groups that are not equal.

Try It Number and Count. Write the number of groups. Write how many are in each group.

1. _2_ groups
_5_ in each group

2. _4_ groups
_2_ in each group

© McGraw-Hill School Division

128 Grade 2, Chapter 14, Cluster A

WHAT IF THE STUDENT CAN'T

Count Groups

- Draw 6 circles on the board and draw lines to divide them into three equal groups. Number the groups and have the student count them. Then draw 8 circles and draw lines to divide them into four equal groups. Have the student number and count the groups. Continue with 10 circles divided into five groups.

Recognize the Meaning of "Equal Groups"

- Place four large rubber bands on a desk or table. Give the student 8 counters and ask him or her to make equal groups in each of the circles. Repeat with 12 counters. Then take away one rubber band and have the student work with 6, 9, and 12 counters.

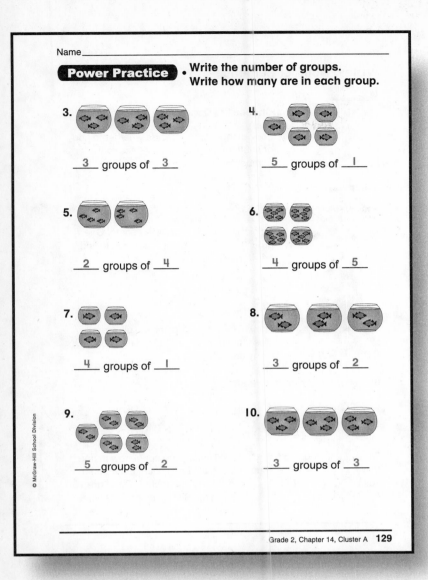

Name_____

Power Practice • Write the number of groups.
Write how many are in each group.

3.   4.

__3__ groups of __3__   __5__ groups of __1__

5.   6.

__2__ groups of __4__   __4__ groups of __5__

7.   8.

__4__ groups of __1__   __3__ groups of __2__

9.   10.

__5__ groups of __2__   __3__ groups of __3__

© McGraw-Hill School Division

Grade 2, Chapter 14, Cluster A **129**

Try It

Remind students that they should count and write the number of groups before they count the number in each group.

Power Practice

• Have students complete the practice items. Then review each answer.

• Discuss how students know that the groups shown are equal. (They have the same number of items.)

Learn with Partners & Parents

Use paper plates and a box of plastic spoons to practice making and counting equal groups.

• Set out 3 plates. Arrange spoons on each plate so that there are equal groups of spoons. How many groups are there? How many spoons are in each group?

• Set out 5 plates. Arrange spoons on each plate so that there are equal groups of spoons. How many groups are there? How many spoons are in each group?

WHAT IF THE STUDENT CAN'T

Complete the Power Practice

• Discuss each incorrect answer. Have the student count the groups aloud before writing the number of groups. Have the student do the same for the number in each group.

Lesson Goal
• Write an addition or subtraction sentence to match a picture.

What the Student Needs to Know
• Recognize plus and minus signs.
• Count objects in an array.

Getting Started
On the board, draw a group of 4 squares and a group of 7 squares. Ask:

• *Would I add or subtract to find how many in all?* (add)

Write: 4 + 7 = 11

Cross out 4 squares. Ask:

• *Would I add or subtract to find how many are left?* (subtract)

Write: 11 – 4 = 7

What Can I Do?
Read the question and the response. Then read and discuss the examples. Ask:

• *What sign do you use to find how many in all?* (a plus sign)

• *What sign do you use to find how many are left?* (a minus sign)

• *When you subtract 6 from 13, what number do you write first?* (13) *Why?* (The greater number comes first in a subtraction sentence.)

Name_____

Write a Number Sentence

Learn

Choose the Operation

Look at the picture. Decide whether to add or subtract. Choose + or – for your number sentence.

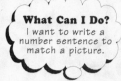 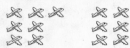

Think: The planes are all the same. One group is joining another. I can add to find how many in all. 7 + 6 = 13

Think: There are 13 planes in all. 6 are crossed out. I can subtract to find out how many are left. 13 – 6 = 7

Use Numbers from the Picture

Think: I can count to find how many in all. One group has 6. One group has 7. 6 + 7 = 13

Think: I can count how many in all. I can count the number being subtracted. There are 13 in all. Six are being subtracted. 13 – 6 = 7

130 Grade 2, Chapter 14, Cluster A

What Can I Do?
I want to write a number sentence to match a picture.

WHAT IF THE STUDENT CAN'T

Recognize Plus and Minus Signs
• Write number sentences with circles in place of the plus and minus signs. For example:

8 ○ 6 = 14; 14 ○ 6 = 8

• Have students supply the signs and read the number sentences aloud.

Count Objects in an Array
• Place two groups of counters on a desk or table. Have the student count the number in each group. Rearrange the counters in an array and have the student count again.

Name_____

Try It • Write a number sentence for each picture.

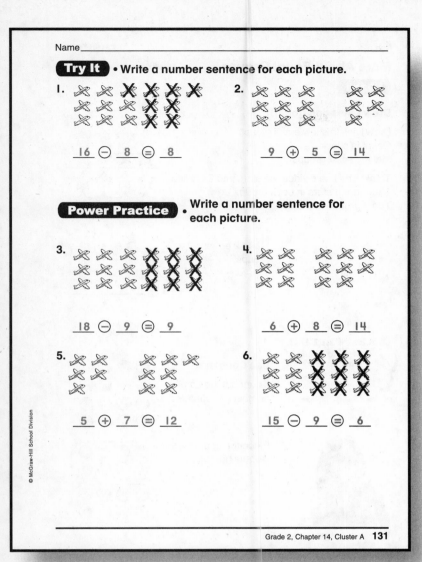

1. 16 ⊖ 8 ⊜ 8

2. 9 ⊕ 5 ⊜ 14

Power Practice • Write a number sentence for each picture.

3. 18 ⊖ 9 ⊜ 9

4. 6 ⊕ 8 ⊜ 14

5. 5 ⊕ 7 ⊜ 12

6. 15 ⊖ 9 ⊜ 6

Grade 2, Chapter 14, Cluster A **131**

Try It

Suggest that students use these steps:

- Choose the operation. Write + or – in the first circle.
- Count the group or groups. Write the numbers on the lines.
- Write = in the second circle.
- Add or subtract and write the answer.
- Check your number sentence against the picture. Does it make sense?

Power Practice

- Remind students to choose the operation first and to use numbers that correspond to the items in the pictures.
- Have students share their work by reading their number sentences aloud.

WHAT IF THE STUDENT CAN'T

Complete the Power Practice

- Have the student explain how he or she would decide whether to add or subtract.

- Discuss each incorrect answer. Have the student count the objects in each picture to check his or her work.

Lesson Goal
- Divide a group into smaller, equal groups.

What the Student Needs to Know
- Recognize the meaning of "equal groups."
- Identify equal groups.

Getting Started
Give each pair of students 16 counters. Say:
- *Make groups of 8. How many groups do you have?* (2)
- *Now, make groups of 4. How many groups do you have?* (4)
- *Make groups of 2. How many groups do you have?* (8)

What Can I Do?
Read the question and the response. Then read and discuss the examples. Ask:
- *How could you divide the balloons into 4 equal groups?* (4 groups of 4) *8 equal groups?* (8 groups of 2)

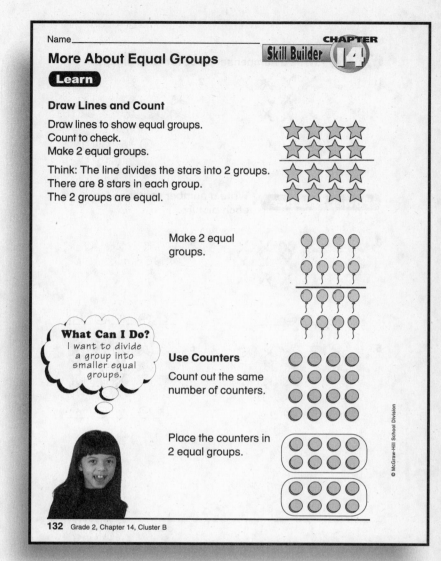

Name_____

More About Equal Groups

Skill Builder CHAPTER 14

Learn

Draw Lines and Count

Draw lines to show equal groups.
Count to check.
Make 2 equal groups.

Think: The line divides the stars into 2 groups.
There are 8 stars in each group.
The 2 groups are equal.

Make 2 equal groups.

What Can I Do?
I want to divide a group into smaller equal groups.

Use Counters
Count out the same number of counters.

Place the counters in 2 equal groups.

© McGraw-Hill School Division

132 Grade 2, Chapter 14, Cluster B

WHAT IF THE STUDENT CAN'T

Recognize the Meaning of "Equal Groups"
- Display 12 counters. Separate them into 2 groups of 6 and have the student tell whether the groups are equal. Repeat with 4 groups of 3; 2 groups of 5 and 1 group of 2; 6 groups of 2; 4 groups of 2 and 1 group of 4; and so on.

Identify Equal Groups
- Provide the student with 12 counters and an egg carton. Have the student show various ways to make equal groups by placing counters in the cups of the egg carton.

Name _____

Try It . Use counters. Then draw lines to show the number of equal groups.

1.

Make 3 equal groups.

2.

Make 4 equal groups.

Power Practice . Draw lines to show the number of equal groups.

3.

Make 2 equal groups.
There are __4__ in each group.

4.

Make 3 equal groups.
There are __3__ in each group.

5.

Make 6 equal groups.
There are __3__ in each group.

6.

Make 5 equal groups.
There are __2__ in each group.

Grade 2, Chapter 14, Cluster B **133**

WHAT IF THE STUDENT CAN'T

Complete the Power Practice

- Discuss each incorrect answer. Have the student model the array pictured with counters. Then give the student a piece of string or yarn to separate the counters into the number of equal groups . Finally, have the student draw the line or lines to show the number of equal groups.

USING THE LESSON

Try It
Remind students that equal groups must have the same number of stars in each.

Power Practice
- Have students complete the practice items. Then review each answer.
- Discuss how students know that the groups they made are equal. (They have the same number of items.)

Lesson Goal
- Identify properties of multiplication.

Introducing the Challenge
- Write the following addition problems on the board and have students name the rule they demonstrate:

$1 + 0 = 1$ $3 + 0 = 3$
$0 + 5 = 5$ $21 + 0 = 21$

(Any number plus 0 equals that number.)

- Then write the following addition problem on the board, and have students identify the rule they demonstrate:

$2 + 3 = 5$ $3 + 2 = 5$
$1 + 8 = 9$ $8 + 1 = 9$

(The order in which you add two numbers does not change the sum.)

Using the Challenge
- Read the directions aloud. Provide counters for students who need them. Point out that students are to write the products and then use those products to formulate a rule.

- When students have solved the problems, discuss the properties of multiplication they discovered. Ask:

- *What would 100 times 0 equal? (0) What would 1,000 times 0 equal? (0)*

- *What would 100 times 1 equal? (100) What would 1,000 times 1 equal? (1,000)*

- *What does 2 times 6 equal? (12) What does 6 times 2 equal? (12)*

Name _____

Find the Rule

Use counters if you need them. Multiply.
Then write the rule.

1. $0 \times 4 =$ __0__ $3 \times 0 =$ __0__ $0 \times 9 =$ __0__

Rule: Any number multiplied by 0 equals __0__.

2. $1 \times 3 =$ __3__ $4 \times 1 =$ __4__ $1 \times 5 =$ __5__

$6 \times 1 =$ __6__ $1 \times 7 =$ __7__ $8 \times 1 =$ __8__

Rule: Any number multiplied by 1 equals <u>itself or that number.</u>

3.

| $\begin{array}{r}5\\ \times 2\\ \hline 10\end{array}$ | $\begin{array}{r}2\\ \times 5\\ \hline 10\end{array}$ | $\begin{array}{r}3\\ \times 4\\ \hline 12\end{array}$ | $\begin{array}{r}4\\ \times 3\\ \hline 12\end{array}$ | $\begin{array}{r}2\\ \times 4\\ \hline 8\end{array}$ | $\begin{array}{r}4\\ \times 2\\ \hline 8\end{array}$ |

| $\begin{array}{r}2\\ \times 3\\ \hline 6\end{array}$ | $\begin{array}{r}3\\ \times 2\\ \hline 6\end{array}$ | $\begin{array}{r}8\\ \times 1\\ \hline 8\end{array}$ | $\begin{array}{r}1\\ \times 8\\ \hline 8\end{array}$ | $\begin{array}{r}7\\ \times 4\\ \hline 28\end{array}$ | $\begin{array}{r}4\\ \times 7\\ \hline 28\end{array}$ |

Write a rule about the order in which you multiply two numbers.
<u>Possible answer: The order in which you multiply</u>
<u>two numbers does not change the answer.</u>

Name_____

Equal Groups in 48

Use 48 counters.
Find all the ways to make equal groups.

___2___ groups of __24__

___3___ groups of __16__

___4___ groups of __12__

___6___ groups of __8__

___8___ groups of __6__

__12__ groups of __4__

__16__ groups of __3__

__24__ groups of __2__

__48__ groups of __1__

© McGraw-Hill School Division

Grade 2, Chapter 14, Cluster B **135**

CHALLENGE

Lesson Goal
• Divide 48 into equal groups.

Introducing the Challenge
• Give each student 6 counters. Say:
• *There are several ways to make equal groups. What are they?* (2 groups of 3, 3 groups of 2, 6 groups of 1)

Using the Challenge
• Read the directions aloud. Give each student or group of students 48 counters.
• Have students complete the activity independently.
• Discuss students' answers and talk about strategies they used to make sure they were including all the possibilities. For example, a logical method would be to increase the number of groups from 2 to 3 to 4 to 5 (which doesn't work) to 6 and so on.